Turning the Tide

An assessment of Baptist Church Growth in England

Paul Beasley-Murray and Alan Wilkinson

Published by Bible Society, 146 Queen Victoria Street,
London EC4V 4BX

BFBS–6M–1981   ISBN 0 564 07062 9

Contents

Preface

I must write this preface with a good bit of conscious restraint and self-control. Paul Beasley-Murray has made such a striking contribution to Church Growth knowledge and literature through the publication of this book that it would be all too tempting to multiply superlatives like galaxies in the Milky Way.

This book, to my knowledge, is a first. Two or three other tests of Church Growth theory have been attempted, but never before has such a thorough empirical test been designed, an instrument applied, and the data processed by computer. This is the most objective, scientific study of Church Growth principles that I have seen. Paul Beasley-Murray and his colleague, Alan Wilkinson, are to be commended for their creativity, skill, and persistence in doing this study and making it available to a wide audience.

I have several specific things I would like to say about this book:

It is a book of faith. This study is not mere intellectual curiosity. It is not rooted in a clever computer program. Rather it is a book which springs from a deep theological conviction. While membership growth in local churches is seen as good and desirable, it is not set forth as an end in itself. The end is the glory of God, and the chief instrument to bring this about is the Holy Spirit. Church Growth is seen as a consequence rather than an objective. Because this is the starting point, the book throughout is positive and optimistic. God is on the throne, working out his will through his servants.

It is a book of courage. Although Paul Beasley-Murray does not mention this, I happen to know that at the beginning he did not receive unanimous approval and support for the project from his colleagues in the ministry. Undaunted, he pushed forward with the study. His burning conviction that 'it is God's plan for his church to grow' is not a popular one in a nation that has been experiencing some decades of steady and alarming church decline. Not only was courage required to express a theological alternative to current intellectual excuses for non-growth, but it was also required on a much more intimate level when Beasley-Murray's own Altrincham Baptist Church was tested against the objective Church Growth criteria he had developed.

It is a book of science. From time to time the book mentions my work on the 'Seven Vital Signs of a Healthy Church'. Paul Beasley-Murray, who is a good personal friend, has correctly interpreted not only the meaning of the signs, but also my intentions in setting them forth. They were, and are, intended to be hypotheses based on the observation of a number of growing churches in America. As hypotheses they are subject to scientific testing, and this book reports on the most extensive test of them to date. Naturally I was gratified that some of them indicate a bias towards growth among Baptist churches in England, and I was also enlightened to read that some of them do not. This study will enable me to go back and adjust my own hypotheses accordingly.

It is a book of discernment. Paul Beasley-Murray is at all times his own person. He is open, he is subject to change his opinions, but he is no captive to the thinking of others. At each crucial point he is able to examine the evidence on

vi

all sides. When the data are clear, he is clear. When the data indicate caution, the interpretation is qualified and tentative. In no sense is he trying to put anything over on the reader. He is not supporting some vested interest.

It is a book of action. Too many Church Growth books (including some of my own) are pure theory with little that a minister finds to be practical. Beasley-Murray has avoided this shortcoming by wisely postponing publication of the results of his research until he had tested them in his own church. Thus, the book not only lays a sound theological and academic foundation, but also it describes the practical outworking of the principles in a specific local parish. Do they work? The graph of growth which had shown a plateauing of church membership in Altrincham began to take an upward turn once again when the church growth principles were incorporated into the church program.

It is a book of challenge. The spiral model for Church Growth which forms a major component of this book is a concrete challenge to church leaders not only in England but elsewhere in the world. More than any other contribution to Church Growth literature that I have seen, the spiral concept integrates internal growth with expansion growth; quality with quantity; perfecting with discipling – to state it in the jargon of the field. It is a new contribution and one which I believe will help hundreds of sluggish churches regain the vision and vitality that God desires for them and enter into a new era of growth.

This book will be a reference point from now on for all serious Church Growth students. I will highly recommend it to students and pastors all over America. My hearty congratulations to Paul Beasley-Murray and Alan Wilkinson for this study and to the Bible Society for making it available to the general public.

C. Peter Wagner
Fuller Theological Seminary
Pasadena, California, U.S.A.

Introduction

There are some questions that a Christian minister hardly dares form into words. To do so would seem almost blasphemous.

I am thinking of those often unspoken issues, like: 'Why do seemingly similar churches fare so differently so far as their growth in numbers is concerned?' 'Why do the most faithful and dedicated local churches often grow less in numbers than those who seem to lack that commitment?' 'Why do two pastors with similar gifts fare so differently in situations which seem much the same?'

In the past, questions such as these have often been designated to the realm of mystery. They have been carefully pigeon-holed under the heading of 'God's Sovereignty' and the Kingdom has continued much the same as before.

But over the past four years, I have had the privilege of carefully forming some of these questions – and more – into words. This has resulted in 350 Baptist churches completing a very detailed questionnaire on their church life. Analysis of their response has turned up some very interesting statistics and led to a fresh set of questions.

The statistics are salutary. We found that, on average, it is taking four church members five years to convert one person. Even those churches that are growing are seeing an average of little more than three people being converted each year. And it is clear that those churches that are growing are generally relying on their new lay leadership being attracted to them from other churches in their area or beyond.

I was also to discover that the size of a congregation has its own effect on whether a church grows or not. So does the number of small-group activities and the way the pastoral responsibilities are shared.

Drawing on the lessons learned from the survey I was then able to put them into practice, with encouraging results.

It has all been a very special privilege, particularly because I have undertaken all this activity in the presence of some very special people. The setting in which this voyage of discovery took place was Altrincham Baptist Church – where over the past eight years some 142 people have been baptized and the church membership has risen from 83 to its present 238. These are far from being impersonal statistics. They represent individuals whom I have grown to love and respect deeply.

My own role in this growth has been no more than to be a mere catalyst in the purposes of God. And I can look back to situations when I made a wrong decision and even hindered the growth of the kingdom.

I am greatly indebted to my colleague Alan Wilkinson. Without him the work in Altrincham would not have developed in the way that it has. This book, though written in the singular, is very much the work of both of us. Without Alan it would certainly never have come into being.

Alan and I are grateful to our wives Irene and Caroline, who have allowed this book – and all that lies behind it – all too often to dominate our lives.

The fact that this book – and the whole story that is in it – leans heavily on statistics makes it immediately suspect to many people. Like the Baptist Union Area Superintendent who wrote chidingly to me when he was asked to co-operate with our survey. He told me, 'I'm never quite sure what people mean by Church Growth. I often find that the most effective churches are those that do not grow numerically. And in personal life real growth is growth into maturity.'

He continued, 'My concept of a near-perfect church is my own last pastorate. Its numbers never increased – or they never seemed to – perhaps because the membership role is revised continuously. Yet here is maturity, relevance and charity. It is a church which continually relates its message and its mission to the community in which it exercises a caring ministry.'

He concluded, 'If anyone was to ask me where they could find the love and grace of Christ I would direct them unhesitatingly to that church. It does not grow in numbers – but I am not sure that we are supposed to. What we are supposed to do is grow in the love and knowledge of Christ. What has the doctrine of the remnant to say to our fevered excitement about numbers?'

Stirring words and they sound so very plausible. But the survey eventually enabled us to look at the statistics that related to the actual church about which he was writing. We found that over the past ten years the membership had declined – from 247 to 231 members.

More significant was the fact that those new members that had been gained were predominantly the result of people transferring from other churches. In one year, when the Superintendent was still the pastor, there were no additions in membership by either baptisms or conversions. But there were 26 additions by transfer. So it is clear that numbers *do* have a contribution to make – as we have been able to prove for ourselves at Altrincham.

What had forced me to begin to vocalize those seemingly 'blasphemous' questions was the fact that the rate of numerical growth that we had been enjoying was noticeably slowing down. The tide was observably on the ebb and I wanted to know why. This led to the research project among Baptist churches, with a particular emphasis on evaluating the major tenets of the Church Growth Movement – particularly in a British setting. The second stage came as we reflected on our findings and led to our developing a unique approach to planning and task-sharing within the life of a church.

Although this had all been done with the situation in Altrincham in mind, I believe that the principles apply to any and every local church.

I am grateful to God that not only have many of my original questions been answered but that the application of the lessons learnt has actually enabled us to see the turning of the tide in our own situation.

Paul Beasley-Murray

Chapter 1

A suitable case for growth?

CALL TO THE NORTH

'Altrincham?' I'd never heard of it. Certainly, it wasn't anywhere that I could easily find on a map. But then I doubt if the residents of Altrincham would have been able to locate Kisangani in Zaire, where I had been lecturing in the theological faculty of the national university for two years. Now that assignment was over and I was looking forward to becoming a minister of an English Baptist church.

The first letter of enquiry I received was from Altrincham. For various reasons, my wife Caroline and I decided that this would not be the right place for us. Nevertheless we went to visit the church. To my surprise there came a growing conviction that this was where God wanted us to be. So in November 1972 we accepted, and on March 3rd 1973 I was inducted to the pastorate of Altrincham Baptist Church.

Altrincham lies to the south-west of Manchester and is the last built-up area before you encounter the glorious Cheshire countryside. Since local government reorganization took place in 1974, the town is officially part of the Metropolitan Borough of Trafford – and thus part of the Metropolitan County of Greater Manchester. Yet the town's postal address remains 'Altrincham, Cheshire' – a fact not without significance. In other words, Altrincham has not become yet another suburb of Manchester. Though many of the town's 48,000 inhabitants commute into the city, they certainly do not consider themselves to be Mancunians.

Altrincham's distinctiveness has been emphasized by the development of a new shopping precinct which includes a number of well-known department stores, together with large versions of popular chain stores. As a result, Altrincham has become a shopping mecca for South Manchester and North Cheshire. It is now, as the advertisements describe it, a regional centre.

Yet, simple as all this sounds, the structure of the town is more complex than you would expect. Altrincham is composed of at least four separate districts or villages: Altrincham, Hale, Bowdon and Timperley. Altrincham proper became a borough in 1290, and for centuries its life was centred around the market place. Its main industrial activity was cotton weaving. This has now been replaced by other industries, particularly light engineering.

Though Bowdon's roots go back to the Domesday Book, the district was really created by 19th century Manchester cotton owners looking for a haven to which to escape from the turmoil of city industry. In the same way, Hale was a product of the railway age and is also considered to be a nice residential area, favoured by executives not least because it is between the airport and the motorway. Timperley on the other hand can be described as a typical middle-class suburban area.

Because of the composite nature of Altrincham, the population itself is mixed. The streets immediately around the Baptist church are rows of small terraced houses in the typical northern industrial style. Yet no more than a mile away is some of the most expensive property imaginable. Indeed, a recent survey revealed parts of Bowdon and Hale to be among the leading districts in the country in terms of the ownership of durable consumer goods.

While Altrincham may have a broad cultural mix across the class range, ethnically it is very unified. There are very few West Indians or Pakistanis, but there is a sizeable Jewish community which has had its own golf course for a good number of years and has recently built its own synagogue.

Friends thought I had done well to be called to what they described as 'the stockbroker belt'. But my own overwhelming impression was of the streets of small terraced houses. Set among them was the Baptist church, at that time a dark and rather dismal building, swathed internally with gallons of brown varnish and not seeming the least attractive in itself. To my mind, it bore a closer resemblance to a disused cotton mill than it did to a place of worship.

IN THE BEGINNING . . .

The church had been founded in 1872, and had experienced a chequered history. Its heyday must have been in the 23 years that ended in 1917. During that time the minister, the Rev Cowell Lloyd, baptized 352 people and built up the membership from 73 to 316. Alas, the growth was not maintained. By 1954 the membership had fallen to 112. Then Dr Jim Perkin became the minister. Under his dynamic leadership the slide was arrested, so that when he left, eight years later, the membership had risen to 130.

Life was not so easy for his successor, the Rev Norman Fairburn. Families began to move out of the area and his congregation started to decline. By the time I arrived, there were only 83 members left. Apart from two married couples under forty years of age, there was a noticeable gap between the Sunday School and the rest of the membership.

Sociologically, church membership reflected the surrounding neighbourhood. There were the wealthy and the less wealthy, the well-educated and the not-so-well educated. And theologically, too, we were a mixed bag with liberals rubbing shoulders with the more conservative evangelicals, of which I am one. There were no charismatics in those early days, though since then some people have become involved in the movement.

If our congregation managed to live together despite its differences, it wasn't wholly due to our building. This had – and indeed still has – some limitations. No doubt the architect treasured dreams of his brick creation as an eternal reminder of late 19th century architecture, but today the building is forbidding rather than imposing. To reach the entrance you must climb the steep stone steps, which are a great physical deterrent to the infirm and a psychological one to many more.

Once inside there is plenty of space overall, though the area for worship is limited and cannot be enlarged any further. The Sunday School room is obstructed by pillars which cannot be moved, and the other rooms are an assortment of sizes spread over several floors, including a basement.

An essential part of understanding Altrincham Baptist Church is to realize that it is virtually the only evangelical church in the town. As a result, it now includes among its members those who were previously from a broad range of denominational persuasions. The other churches with an evangelical stance are two small Brethren assemblies and a small but apparently growing Pentecostal church in Bowdon. The church has accordingly a particular contribution to make to the Christian life of the town, apart from its own denominational witness.

THE WAY AHEAD?
When Caroline and I came to take up our responsibilities in the church in March 1973, we brought no carefully worked out strategy with us. We did, however, have one clear goal: to use 'all means' to win men and women for Jesus Christ. Even before I had actually been inducted, a letter was circulated around the neighbourhood which announced, 'Dr Beasley-Murray has now come to serve the community in Altrincham. He believes that Jesus Christ is

4

the ultimate answer to man's need and he is anxious that you too might come to know this.'

From the beginning the church responded actively to the challenge. We held our first guest service at Easter, only weeks after our arrival. It became the first of a series that included contributions from gifted people as varied as Rodney Macann, the New Zealand bass-baritone, and Professor F F Bruce of Manchester's Faculty of Theology.

To complement this evangelistic activity, we set to work on giving the church interior some cosmetic surgery in order to make it more attractive and welcoming. The sanctuary was opened up and the pastel colours changed to sunnier hues, bringing a feeling of space and friendliness to the interior. A new glass porch made the entrance seem a little more welcoming. We changed the time of the morning service from 11 a.m. to 10.15 a.m. and started having tea in the school room after morning service, thus giving an extra opportunity for a welcome to develop into fellowship.

Meanwhile, the emphasis on evangelism continued. In the autumn of 1973 my wife, together with other ladies in the church, began a Ladies' Coffee Evening. It was one of the most important steps we took. It attracted ladies of an age group younger than most of those in membership and through them we also began to contact their husbands.

This began to affect the composition of our congregation, as did the rekindling of interest in youth work. An enthusiastic couple joined the church and helped establish a Sunday evening Youth Fellowship. This was so successful that the following spring we began a regular coffee evening. Droves of young people came along from the local schools and many of them came to a real faith.

But we felt the need for something more. We had been actively involved in the Stephen Olford Crusade which had taken place in Platt Fields, Manchester, some eight miles away, and in the summer of 1974 we organized our own campaign for evangelism. A team of students, many of them members of The Robert Hall Society, the Baptist

Society for students of Cambridge University, came to Altrincham. They conducted a programme of house visits which formed part of a Community Religious Survey. Now, six years later, there are still five families in the church who date their Christian beginnings from that time.

Our work received another tremendous boost in September 1977 when about thirty-five students from Spurgeon's College helped us mount a full-scale evangelistic mission. Using the slogan *Faith for Today* we presented the Gospel in a variety of ways. Along with a religious survey of some 5,000 homes, we held lectures on Christian basics, ran about 40 informal coffee groups, sponsored two Gospel concerts, showed the film *The Cross and the Switchblade*, did street theatre in the local shopping precinct . . . You name it, we did it!

Apart from the directly evangelistic impact generated by all this activity, it also increased the community's awareness of the church. This was further helped when Granada TV televised a baptismal service from the church in May 1976, and more recently when BBC Radio 4 broadcast our Morning Service to the homes of many within Altrincham and beyond.

THE DOUBTS BEGIN

Throughout this time I was privileged to see the church growing, both in maturity in Christ and particularly in the numbers being converted and asking to become members. Yet, five years after our arrival, I found myself struggling with a conviction that things were not really as they should be.

In those five years, the membership of the church had more than doubled. But now I could see that the rate of growth we had been enjoying was beginning to slow down. All the same activities continued – and more. Yet I knew that they were not making the same impact that they had before.

The Lord Jesus Christ was never afraid to use business imagery in order to communicate what he had to say. Many of his parables were about management and involved stewardship, wages, buying, selling and husbandry. So I felt myself to be on safe ground as I spoke to the Church Members Annual General Meeting in April 1978, telling them that I considered the gathering to be the equivalent of a business company's annual stocktaking.

'Just as a company expects to see returns on the investments and energy it has expended,' I explained, 'so should we be looking for the results of our Christian service.'

I could see from the statistics of our church (Fig. 1) that despite five great years of progress things were beginning to plateau off. In 1973 we had 87 members; in 1974, 95 members; in 1975, 116 members; in 1976, 150 members; in 1977, 170 members; and in 1978, 180 members. The larger the church grew the more effort it was taking to give pastoral care to those in membership while trying also to reach out with the good news of Jesus Christ.

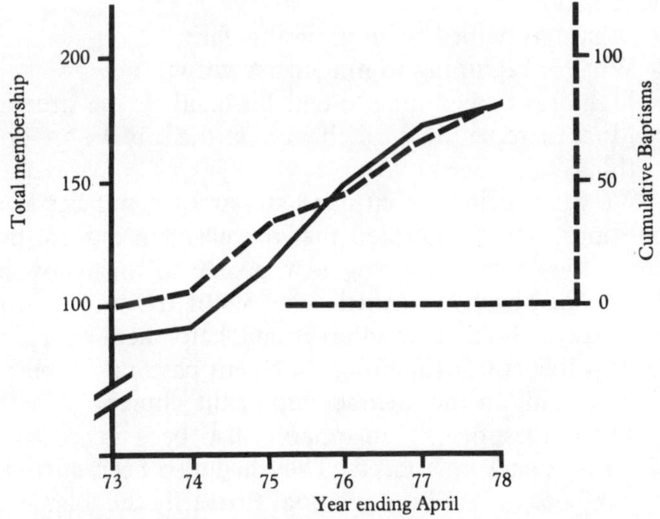

Fig. 1 Membership and cumulative baptisms by years

Facing the church meeting with the facts, I also pointed out that, 'This past year it has taken 170 of us to add 10 others to our number – and even some of these have transferred to us from churches in other areas.'

In addition we were up against the bath plug phenomenon. When the taps are full on and the plug is out, you waste water. And we were wasting people. We were seeing a good flow of new people joining us but others were transferring to other local churches, and while they gave theological grounds for doing so, in reality the governing factors may have been sociological. The mix we had found so valuable was now proving a problem. As the congregation grew, people began to feel less and less happy with those from different streams of society and became less involved in church life. So, like water in a bath, they were swept away.

And it seemed as though I could do nothing to stop them leaving. The church had doubled in five years but now the growth was slowing down again. How could this be? Nagging questions kept coming into my mind and into our deliberations:

- What has helped us to grow this far?
- What is beginning to hinder our growth now?
- Is the Lord beginning to take his hand off the situation?
- Must there be practical changes in the way we are doing things?

We were seeing a continued stream of new faces at our meetings, which indicated that the problem did not lie in any difficulty of attracting new people to the fellowship. Later, the struggle seemed to be about the way in which we were to hold their interest and help them to a living faith, while still maintaining sufficient pastoral support for those already in the membership of the church.

These questions – and others – had been raised by the situation that I now faced. They had also been stirred up by the books I had been reading. Primarily the 'blame' can be laid at the feet of the book *Your Church Can Grow* by Peter Wagner (Regal Books 1976). It introduced me to some mind-stretching concepts, and to a new piece of Christian jargon – *Church Growth*.

Chapter 2

Not only for America

MORE QUESTIONS AND SOME OF THE ANSWERS
Why do some spiritual and prayerful churches grow, while others do not? Why do two equally faithful and gifted men have such vastly different results to their ministry? Why are some denominations growing and others not? Is God picking and choosing? If so, why does he sometimes pass over those with the most orthodox doctrines and deepest commitment?

These questions have furrowed many brows, though to a large extent they remain unspoken. In fact, we are inclined to shrug our shoulders and get on with the work, believing that this is all part of the great mystery of God's plan.

These nagging questions – and others like them – *are* of prime interest to a missionary seeking to establish a work in a foreign land. Such a man was Donald McGavran, a third generation missionary with thirty years' service in India. He was moved to discover answers to these questions and his research has had interesting results. It has given rise to a whole new school of thought which believes that the roots of these problems lie in the practical and sociological factors which make up our society. The general banner under which this thinking is now expounded is the phrase Church Growth, which has more content to it than those who encounter it for the first time may realize.

When Donald McGavran set about finding answers, he used scientific methodology. Pure science involves observation and analysis. McGavran borrowed these techniques, looking at churches and identifying the vital issues which appeared to be contributing to their growth. Nevertheless, in spite of this emphasis on science, Donald McGavran does not suggest that the factors contributing to growth can be reduced to a simple formula. He insists that Church Growth is a complex matter. To illustrate the fact he tells of an interview he had with the pastor of a growing church. The man gave his own assessment of the reason for the growth as being, 'We preach the Bible as the word of God and are faithful to it.' But Donald McGavran goes on to tell of interviewing another pastor whose church had remained stagnant through ten years and who gave his assessment of the situation as, 'We preach the Bible as the word of God and are faithful to it.'

The Church Growth Movement sees answers such as these as being superficial in the extreme. They do not argue with the fact of the Bible being the basis of the Church's life – indeed they support this – but they are wary of over-emphasizing one single factor. Too often they feel churches operate in a fog with no one knowing what is working and what is not. The whole social dimension can easily be ignored. So McGavran and his followers lay stress on gathering factual information and actually measuring what has been done. They call it 'membership accounting'.

McGavran sees the role of assessing a church as being rather like a doctor diagnosing a sick patient. How can a cure be prescribed until the disease has been discovered?

He began to share his thinking on the subject through several books and articles published in the late 1950s – which eventually led to his founding the Institute of Church Growth in Eugene, Oregon, in 1961. Four years later this

10

moved to become part of the prestigious Fuller Theological Seminary, in Pasadena, California.

Although the original aim of the Institute was to train people for work overseas as missionaries, spreading the Gospel and planting new churches, McGavran began to revise his ideas. By the early 1970s, he was convinced that the principles being taught applied just as much to America itself.

While Donald McGavran could justifiably be described as the father of the Church Growth Movement, Peter Wagner, another professor at Fuller Theological Seminary, has been one of its major exponents. He insists, 'It is simply biblical and theological nonsense to argue that God is pleased with churches, year after year, generation after generation, who lose members.' (*Your Church Can Grow*).

IF THEY CAN DO IT . . .

That conviction is beginning to grip the church in Britain, and the news that growth is possible has resulted in fresh waves of buoyant optimism breaking out in many areas of church life.

Then the movement received world-wide impetus through the International Congress on World Evangelization held at Lausanne, Switzerland in 1974. Another major step forward for Britain came through the *Let My People Grow* initiative of 1976, when three evangelical organizations (the Evangelical Alliance, the Billy Graham Evangelistic Association, and the Church of England Evangelical Council) set up a working group to make plans for a major evangelistic initiative.

Church Growth thinking so permeated this working group that it came out with an imaginative objective to 'treble the number of convinced Christians in the country by 1980, and to have at least 5% active, informed Christians in every segment of society'. The report failed to gain support but it did put the subject of Church Growth firmly on the agenda of church life in Britain, particularly as far as those at leadership level were concerned.

The Church Growth banner is presently being vigorously waved by the Bible Society, who have a department devoted to teaching Church Growth principles through special workshops. The Evangelical Alliance has also established its own Church Growth unit.

Probably the most important contribution that the Church Growth Movement has made to church life in Britain has been the injection of a new mood of confidence. British Christians have been shown a new vision of the Church rising phoenix-like from the ashes of at least two decades of depression. The Church is beginning to break free from an almost subconscious commitment to a belief that it is not even God's plan for the Church in Britain to grow.

Faced with a predominant pattern of churches *not* growing, there has been a tendency to construct a defence to justify the situation. Phrases like 'quality not quantity' and 'small is beautiful' have accompanied the assertion that we are now in a post-Christian age. Therefore we must hang on to the end. In fact, we have become like the beleaguered troops in so many third-rate cowboy films. We fall to the onslaught of the enemy forces as we wait optimistically for the relief column to come galloping over the horizon.

A TRIANGULAR BASE

But the mood is changing and Peter Wagner has summed it up under three headings – obedience, pragmatism and optimism. They make a useful summary of the philosophy of the Church Growth Movement.

Obedience

Church Growth thinking is directly related to an obedient response to the Great Commission recorded in Matthew 28.18–20. The Lord Jesus Christ tells his disciples, 'I have been given all authority in heaven and on earth. Go, then, to all peoples everywhere and make them my disciples: baptize them in the name of the Father, the Son, and the Holy Spirit, and teach them to obey everything I have commanded you. And I will be with you always, to the end of the age.' This is so important to Church Growth thinking that Peter Wagner makes sure he has a constant reminder of it. The American registration system allows people to have personalized number plates on their cars so Wagner can choose whether he drives MT 2819 or MT 2820. What discipline it must take not to buy another car in order to give it the registration number MT 2818 and so complete the theological picture!

Obedience to this Great Commission, according to Church Growth thinking, involves four particular factors:

- growth in numbers
- maturity of believers
- pragmatism
- optimism.

The first century church experienced *growth in numbers* at an amazing rate. In the first chapter of the Book of Acts we read of 120 people gathered in an upper room. That day ended with some 3,000 more having been added to their number – though not, we hasten to add, in the same upper room! From then on there was no stopping the growth of the Church. As Acts 2.47 tells us: 'And every day the Lord added to their group.'

In Acts 4.4 we read of 5,000 men believing – a figure that apparently did not include women or children, and by Acts 6.7 Luke gives up figures altogether. He tells us that 'the number of disciples grew larger and larger'. So it is no exaggeration to describe the Acts of the Apostles as a record of Church Growth. Indeed the Book of Acts abounds in references to growth. Take a look at 6.1; 9.31–42; 11.21; 12.24; 13.49; 16.5; 19.20; 21.20.

The Church Growth Movement rests its case on the basic belief that the Church today should also grow. More than that, its exponents say, it is actually God's plan, will and purpose that it should do so.

Unfortunately, few local churches feature the concept of growth as part of their agenda. In some cases this is because the church may not be as genuinely enthusiastic about growing as it would have those outside believe. The pastor may subconsciously feel that he has enough problems to contend with already. Alternatively the members may be resistant to growth, feeling nicely settled together in a cosy fellowship situation and, therefore, subconsciously resistant to any new people who would disturb the present ease and comfort they are enjoying.

Another reason, as Peter Wagner has explained, is that there may be 'an undue stress on Christian perfection. That can turn a congregation into spiritual navel-gazers, who are so pleased with their own heroic attainments that they have little tolerance for newer Christians who are not as polished.' As a result they are like middle-aged married couples who do not want the inconvenience of babies around the house. Spiritually speaking, they are on the pill. This, says Church Growth thinking, is an attitude that is in direct disobedience to God's plan and purpose: the Church should be 'fruitful and multiply'.

However, Church Growth protagonists insist that obedience involves more than just a slavish quest for numbers. *Maturity in Christ* (Ephesians 4.11–16; Colossians 1.28) is of equal importance to growth in numbers. This concept can be seen within the context of the Great Commission just as clearly as can the multiplication process of new believers being added to the Church.

Church Growth leaders make a clear distinction between the function of actually adding numbers of new disciples and what really happens to those new disciples once they have been added. These two steps are referred to as *discipling* and *perfecting*. Both are equally present in the task set before the Church in the Great Commission. *Discipling* is seen in the command 'make disciples . . . baptize them,' while *perfecting* is implicit in the command to 'make disciples . . . teach them.'

Obedience also involves taking the local church seriously. It would seem that in recent decades, much of the effort of evangelicals has been focussed outside the local church. Energy and expertise have been channelled into what have become known as para-church organizations. These are as diverse as youth movements, publishing houses and evangelistic societies and include such organizations as Scripture Union, the Evangelical Alliance and Inter-Varsity Press. The Church Growth Movement reverses this trend, making it a priority for a person to express his commitment to Christ through also being committed to a local church. Para-church organizations should only exist, say Church Growth people, in order to benefit the local church and those organizations would probably agree.

Obedience also touches on the kind of evangelism that should happen. We are not called to shout from a distance but to position ourselves in our hearers' presence just as Jesus came into our world to make himself known to us. The pattern of Christ's incarnation should be present in our own approach to evangelism.

Pragmatism
By its own definition, the Church Growth Movement makes use of the 'best insights of contemporary social and behavioural sciences'. Factual statistical data are essential in any analysis or situation. It is on this that *pragmatic decisions* are made.

Not that there is any suggestion that statistical data in themselves can promote growth. Rather, it is that the careful analysis and interpretation of the right data can pinpoint factors which may be hindering or helping the life of the church.

One way in which the Movement uses the data is to diagnose a wide range of 'illnesses' that can affect the health of any local church. A very perceptive application of this principle in a British context can be found in a helpful book by Eddie Gibbs, *Body Building Exercises for the Local Church* (Falcon, London 1979).

Church Growth thinkers also look for signs of health. Peter Wagner has made much of what he calls the *Seven Vital Signs* which contribute to a church growing. These Seven Vital Signs provide the backbone of *Your Church*

Can Grow. He argues that the factors likely to be present in churches which are growing are:

- The attitude and authority of the minister.
- The effective mobilization of the lay members.
- The variety of programme and facilities of the church.
- The relationship between members in both congregational activities and in smaller groups.
- Basically one kind of people in the church.
- The use of evangelistic methods that have already been proved to be effective.
- The need to put evangelism and care of new converts as a higher priority than social action.

Essentially all these vital signs are the result of wondering what sort of action should be taken. But sometimes too much attention is paid to the action and not enough to prayerful study of the problem and a biblically-based strategy which takes God's plans into account as well as man's. People often seem content to play the numbers game alone, ignoring that the Lord himself is behind any true movement for growth and that all such ventures should be grounded in him.

Optimism
Despite the Movement's emphasis on techniques and statistics, these are not the basis for the *optimism* it demands. The confidence of the Church Growth Movement is in the person of Jesus and his great promise in Matthew 16.18: 'I will build my church'. It is *Christ's* Church and he is building it. We have merely been invited to become part of his team and to work with him in building something about which he has promised 'not even death will ever be able to overcome it'.

Such optimism results not from belief in the power of grids and graph paper but in the power of a sovereign God. Consequently, the Church Growth Movement places great emphasis on faith. It was Paul Harvey who once said, 'A blind man's world is bounded by the limits of his touch;

an ignorant man's world by the limits of his knowledge; a great man's world by the limits of his vision.'

This makes some words of the great missionary pioneer, William Carey, utterly contemporary: 'Expect great things from God. Attempt great things for God.' Significantly, William Carey was also interested in Church Growth and his statistical data can be read in his celebrated pamphlet, known as *The Enquiry*.

The combination of faith and pragmatism has led the Church Growth Movement to express specific visions in quantifiable terms. In other words, they look for Church Growth goals which are achievable by faith and can be specifically measured. For example, it is not enough for a church simply to define its aim as 'to reach others'. They want to know how many others. And during what period of time.

Peter Wagner speaks for the whole Movement when he criticizes those churches which employ fail-safe methods by not setting objectives. He says that it is like 'the marksman who shoots a bullet in the wall and then draws a target around the bullet hole.' Thus he encourages churches to set a minimum goal for a growth rate of 25% in a decade, whereas a good aim would be 100% over that period.

I find no theological problems with this optimistic approach. Ours is not the age for a remnant theology. God's intention is to reconcile the world to himself and the cross is the basis of our optimism. The evil one has been defeated; Jesus is Lord; we have his Spirit. 'If God is for us, who can be against us?' (Romans 8.31). Optimism can indeed be justified!

Although that is a good expression of the way I feel today, I wasn't quite so optimistic in August 1977. At that time I had already been experiencing an awareness that the encouraging growth at Altrincham was beginning to lose momentum. Then came a throw-away remark at a Baptist Union Committee meeting that I was attending. Someone suggested that we ought to be paying attention to what the

Americans were discovering about Church Growth, and he recommended Peter Wagner's book.

It made impressive reading during my summer holiday in North Wales that year. It was a particular help to find some clues to explain why the growth at Altrincham had taken place. But it also raised questions. Was there more to it than that? Could his Seven Vital Signs provide the key to enable our growth to continue rather than wane? Or could Church Growth thinking be translated into British culture at all?

Chapter 3

Where do we go from here?

So Church Growth could be genuinely exciting, but how was it related to the British culture? And, more specifically, how was it related to the problems of Altrincham Baptist Church? I had to find out – and through the Lord's timing, I was able to do just that. Baptist ministers are encouraged to take a two to three month break every eight years. I was just coming up to this sabbatical leave and had planned to continue my New Testament studies in Switzerland. But then it seemed a better use of my time to do something of more direct relevance to me as a pastor and thus help our church. And what better field to explore than the relevance of Church Growth principles to the British situation in general, and to Altrincham Baptist Church in particular?

But first of all I needed a greater understanding of Peter Wagner's ideas and methods and the obvious way to get this was to spend some time in the United States. In 1977, I was able to arrange a pulpit exchange with the minister of the Peachtree Baptist Church in Atlanta, Georgia, though before taking this up, I went to Detroit to a seminar run by Wagner and the Fuller Theological Seminary. Both these experiences were to give me a good grounding in my subject. Detroit filled me in on theory and Atlanta, the headquarters of the Home Mission Board of the Southern Baptists, was to help on the practical side. Here I was able to meet church leaders and discuss with them the problems of Church Growth. They had already carried out a survey based on Peter Wagner's Seven Vital Signs and their experiences and findings were to provide me with important help and information.

Before leaving for America, I too had embarked on a survey. My own concern had been to complement my fact-finding mission with a serious evaluation of Peter Wagner's Seven Vital Signs as they related to the life of English churches, and had planned a questionnaire along the lines of the American ones. However, I had been additionally concerned that Wagner's own work and indeed that of the Southern Baptists had been exclusively with those churches which were actually growing. The same in-depth investigation had not been carried out in churches with a static or falling membership. This was something I wanted to explore.

Obviously I wanted to have the results of my questionnaire to take with me to Atlanta, and in preparing them and indeed this book I was helped by one of my deacons, Alan Wilkinson. He used to work in chemical industry but is now Senior Fellow (Administration) of the Manchester Business School. Much of the complicated statistical work was to fall to him.

We discussed the project in November 1977 and realized that we had only seven months in which to complete it. With this time limitation, we could see that a single, wide-ranging postal questionnaire was the only method open to us. Any attempt to take the research in sections, each building on the results of earlier inquiries, or to involve in-depth interviews of some of the respondents, was clearly not going to be possible.

WHAT QUESTIONS SHOULD WE ASK?
In designing the questionnaire, we took an early decision
to obscure the fact that its purpose was to test the hypotheses of Wagner's Seven Vital Signs in a British context,
for Church Growth is a topic about which some people take
a firm stance. In this way we hoped to eliminate any bias
by being vague as to our apparent objective. We worked at
making it a general questionnaire on church life. (The full
questionnaire is reproduced as Appendix 2).

We wanted to generate questions which, without being
leading, would enable us to make fair suppositions about
the validity of Wagner's views. Help came from various
quarters, but in particular we were fortunate to have Do-
rothy Mercer, a Research Fellow at the Manchester Business School and very experienced in the design of
questionnaires and their analysis. As a committed Christian
she was more than willing to work with us on formulating
the questions we were to ask.

Working with a specimen questionnaire we tried to eliminate any ambiguities and imprecision in the English. Then
a trial run was done at a conference with ministers of about
15 churches. Having incorporated the lessons learnt from
this pilot study the questionnaire was ready.

WHICH CHURCHES SHOULD WE CONTACT?
A second factor which caused us a good deal of concern
was how to select the churches to which the questionnaire
should be sent. We were looking for a representative and
statistically valid sample. Faced with the knowledge that
the membership of the Baptist Union has been in decline
for most of the century, we felt it important to make sure
that the sample included churches that were actually growing. In an attempt to unearth them, we asked the Baptist
Union Area Superintendents to provide names of churches
which they felt fulfilled these criteria. They suggested about
a hundred names.

But we needed a broader sample. We found the extra
churches for our list by going through the Baptist Hand-

book for England and taking each alternate church which had a membership in excess of 50. This ensured that the overall sample would be geographically representative. (See Appendix 3, which gives the geographic distribution of the sample.) Fortunately the responses, too, came from all over the country.

We had decided to concentrate on churches with 50 or more members, so that our research could try to equate the American Church Growth proposition that a fellowship should be large enough to provide an adequate range of activities for the needs of both the members and the wider community.

CRACKING THE CODES
Nearly two-thirds of the churches completed the questionnaires – an astonishing response rate for a postal survey, especially one of such complexity. We had much for which to be grateful in the care and attention with which the forms were completed.

Coding the questionnaires ready for the computer was an exhausting process, involving over 600 man hours. Alan had the main task but he was helped out by about twenty-five members of the congregation. It wasn't simply a matter of filling in cards. They had to learn how to code and complete the forms so that the cards could be punched. We ended up with 300,000 items of information readily accessible on the computer. They provide details of the life of 330 Baptist churches in England which have a current membership of over 50. It is probably the most comprehensive data base available on any denomination in any country. Our initial fears were that by including churches that Area Superintendents had designated as growing we would distort the overall sample. We were to discover that some Superintendents had put forward churches which were not growing at all in numerical terms and had failed to supply many of the churches which were.

We were particularly conscious of this possibility of distortion when the first major finding came as a surprise. Six out of every ten of the churches in our sample had grown over the past two years. This was in the face of the Baptist Denomination as a whole being in slight numerical decline. Our immediate fear was that in some way the sample had been unbalanced. If that was the case, it would invalidate our whole survey. So, using statistics from the Baptist Handbook we checked the other churches with over 50 members and also those under 50 in a number of areas. The other churches over 50 showed a similar proportion of growing churches but we discovered that those with a membership under 50 are losing twice the number that those over 50 are gaining. The bath plug phenomena was at work again!

The second major conclusion to be reached was that the productivity of the churches in the sample was abysmal in terms of winning people to Christ. It was disheartening to find churches with huge activity and yet no conversions, and Baptist churches which had seen no baptisms in the ten years under review.

On average it was taking four church members five years to convert just one person. Even in the so-called growing churches, on average, no more than 16 people were being won for Christ in a five-year period.

Of course, there is more to Church Growth than simply adding numbers. As a pastor I am as much concerned to see people mature in the faith as for them to be won for Christ. Quality is as important as quantity. Indeed without spiritual growth there will be no numerical growth. But surely the opposite is also true.

Of necessity our survey was limited to assessing numerical growth, primarily because it is almost impossible to produce a genuinely measurable assessment of the quality of spiritual growth.

But, right at the beginning, we had to establish what we meant by growth. We asked each church to give the number in the fellowship 10 years ago, five years ago, two years ago and at the present time. A church was considered to be growing if it had been adding to its numbers over the whole period or if the figures had shown an upturn at the five year and two year landmarks. For the purpose of computer programming we gave each one of the possible growth trends a number, as illustrated. (Fig. 2)

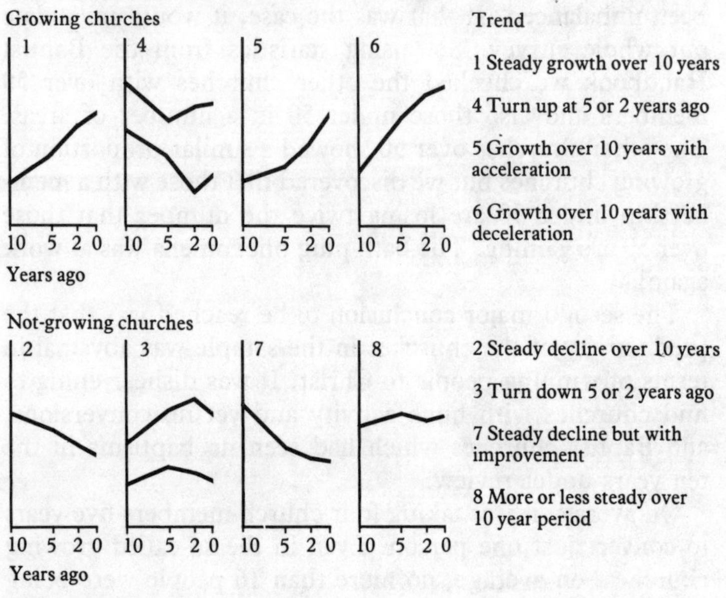

Fig. 2 Growth trends

Of the churches in the Trend 4 group, there are those which only show growth over the past two years. These are statistically suspect since it is possible that some of them may have shown an increase simply through a delay in reviewing their membership roll, or by some other local accident of circumstances. But such churches only represent some 15% of the overall sample.

The discovery that 60% of the total number of churches were growing while 40% were not, gave an average figure for the whole group. With this average as a base, we began looking for factors where the number of churches in the sample exhibiting that factor varied from the average. Where a number of churches that were linked together by a common factor had more than 60% of their number

24

growing, this factor was considered to produce a bias towards growth.

Before telling what we learned about the Vital Signs, some background would be useful. It is important to understand exactly what is meant by a bias towards growth. Simply it is finding the average percentage of churches which are moving in one direction and then comparing the figures of a survey under a specific heading. If the overall average is 60% and the survey yields a percentage of 62 for that heading, it can be said that there is a bias above the average towards growth. This will mean that 38% will not be growing. Let us look at some examples.

When we looked at churches in an inner-city environment we found that 55% were not growing. Thus we can say that inner-city churches have a greater than average bias towards not growing. This can be expressed as 15%, that is to say the specific figure for the area (55%) less the average figure (40%).

In contrast, the churches situated in rural areas were found to have 67% of their number growing. This is 7% above the average of 60% for the total survey. This means that churches in rural areas can be said to have a bias towards growth.

Or take another example. Those churches whose congregation consisted mainly of local people had 63% of their number growing. This indicated a slight bias towards growth. Again churches whose congregation was mainly non-local had almost 61% of their number not growing. As the average number of churches in the survey who were not growing was 40%, this means that churches whose congregation is mainly non-local have a 21% bias towards not growing.

This can be illustrated in diagram form by showing the percentage above average growth on top of a given line and the percentage below average growth below the same line. Fig. 3 shows this in relation to the composition of congregations. But this needs to be interpreted sensibly. It would appear to have as much to do with where the congregation themselves come from as to where the church building is actually situated.

Where a church congregation is made up of half local people with the other half coming from surrounding areas, there is no particular bias one way or another, no matter where it is.

But where the congregation is non-local, and these tend to be city-centre churches, there is a very strong bias towards not growing. These are situations where many have moved out to the suburbs either through redevelopment or through economic choice. But some members are still staying in fellowship with their original congregation, driving back on a Sunday. (Fig. 3)

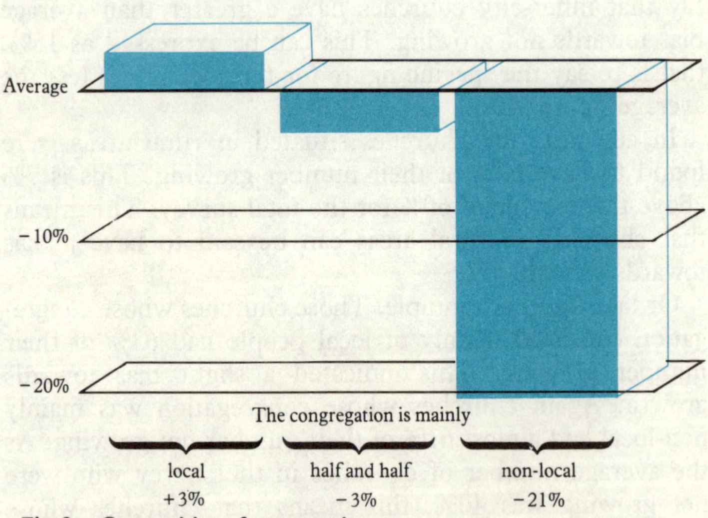

Fig. 3   Composition of congregation

There emerged a very clear pattern of growth in terms of where a church was located. As can be seen from Fig. 4, there is a definite trend towards growth as the church moves from the inner city to a rural location, though it must be stressed that we are only talking about a bias towards growth. So, even in the inner city, 45% of churches

26

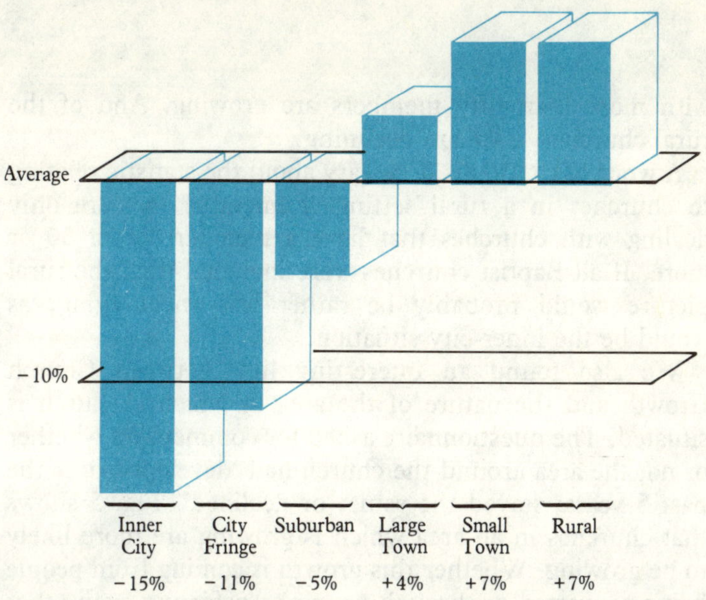

Fig. 4 Location of church

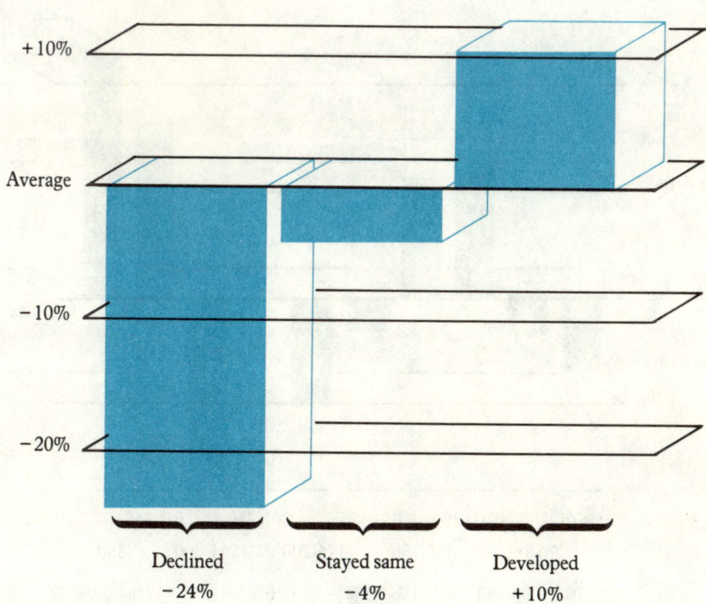

Fig. 5 How has the locality changed over the last five years?

with more than fifty members are growing. And of the rural churches, 33% are declining.

A word of caution is necessary about the statistic relating to churches in a rural setting. Remember, we are only dealing with churches that have a membership of 50 or more. If all Baptist churches were included then the rural picture would probably be rather less encouraging, as would be the inner-city situation.

We also found an interesting link between Church Growth and the nature of the area in which a church is situated. The questionnaire asked for comment on whether or not the area around the church had 'developed over the past 5 years; stayed the same; or declined'. Fig. 5 shows that churches in an area which is growing are more likely to be growing. Whether this growth is coming from people being converted or through people transferring from other churches is something we will consider later on.

A last general diagram relates the tendency for growth to the size of membership of the church. As you will see

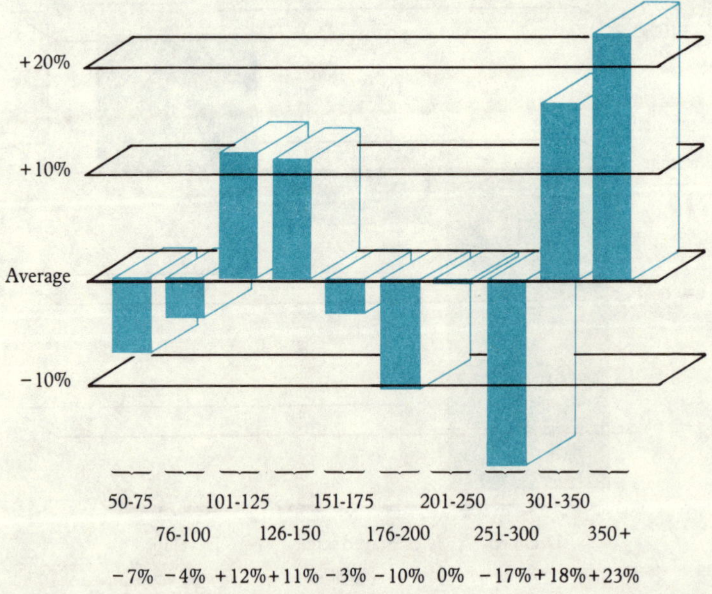

Fig. 6   Church membership

28

from Fig. 6 churches are more likely to be growing in two bands of membership size, '101 – 150' and '301 and over'. This so paralleled the Altrincham experience of rapid growth and then slowing down at 170 – 180 members. It also was in broad agreement with the work by David Wasdell on the Church of England. (Fig. 6)

In some ways this reinforced my concern for our slowing down. Presumably those churches with over 300 members had found some answers, so with those factors as a background it was possible to begin to test Peter Wagner's Seven Vital Signs of Church Growth.

HIGH WATERMARKS
- 60% of Baptist churches in England with membership in excess of 50 have grown in recent years.
- Much of this growth has been by transfer, the average rate of conversions per church has been low, although it is an average over a wide spread of figures.
- The area in which a church is located and the size of the church membership affect growth.

Chapter 4

Unpacking the power

WHAT DIFFERENCE DOES THE MINISTER MAKE?
The key person in a growing church is the pastor, according to Peter Wagner. He is 'the primary catalytic factor for growth'. Thus the first of the Vital Signs of a growing church is, 'a pastor who is a possibility thinker and whose dynamic leadership has been used to catalyze the entire church into action for growth.'

Before looking at the factors which relate directly to that statement, some general comments on the qualities of the ministers in our sample need to be made. A pastor, of course, cannot make a church grow all by himself. He needs others. However, he must provide the key gift of leadership and this is the point which Peter Wagner is principally trying to make.

'PASTOR, DON'T BE AFRAID OF YOUR POWER'
Peter Wagner uses this as a heading in his book and I can still recall the shudder that I felt when first I read it. My very title of minister constantly reminds me that I am called to serve others rather than to exercise power. But Wagner makes the point that the very best service a pastor can render to his people is the service of leadership.

31

With this in mind, we have used the survey to ask a whole range of questions relevant to the personality and role of the minister (see Appendix 2) – some immediately pertinent to Wagner's Vital Sign.

First we focussed on the minister's age (Fig. 7), length of service in the ministry (Fig. 8), and length of service in his present church (Fig. 9). With regard to the minister's age and his length of service in the ministry generally, it is clear that a man in his thirties who has only served about 5 to 10 years in the ministry is the one most likely to experience growth. Energy rather than experience may be the premium.

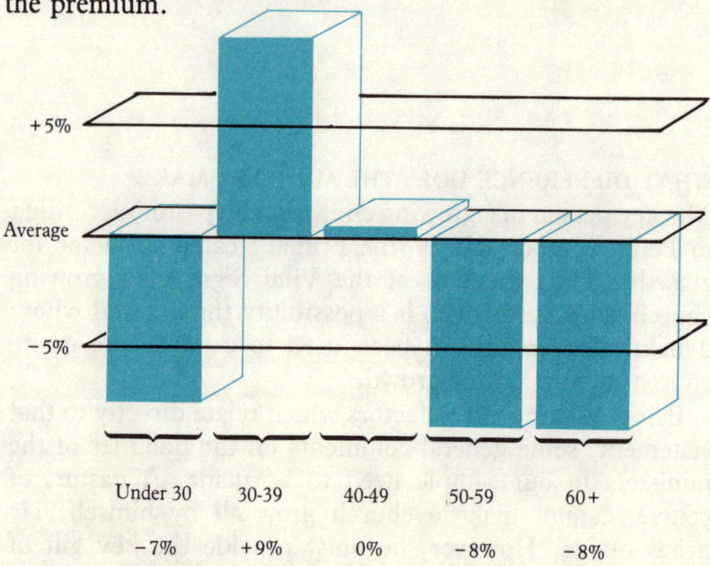

Fig. 7   Age of minister

However, it is dangerous to draw strong conclusions, particularly when no minister can be responsible for his age. Nor can he have much control over how long he has been in the ministry. What is more, it is possible to have a minister who, taking the worst aspects of these statistics, is over 60, has been in the ministry 25 years, and yet still has a growing church.

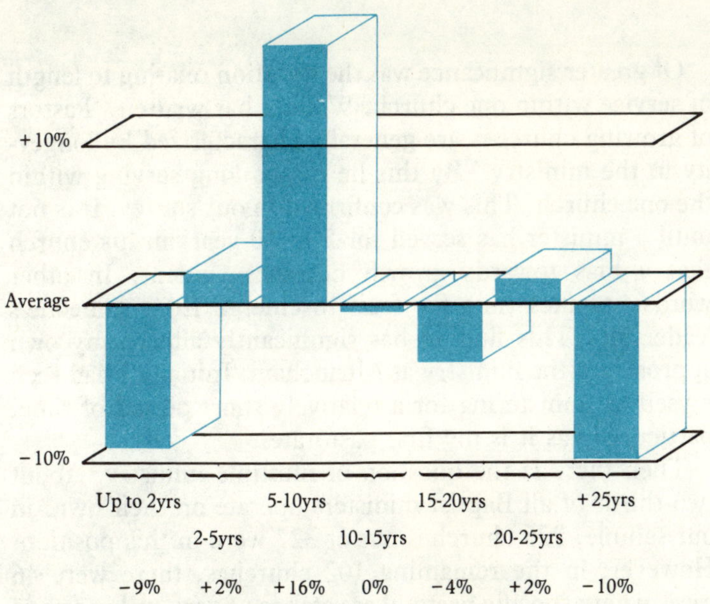

Fig. 8   Length of service in ministry

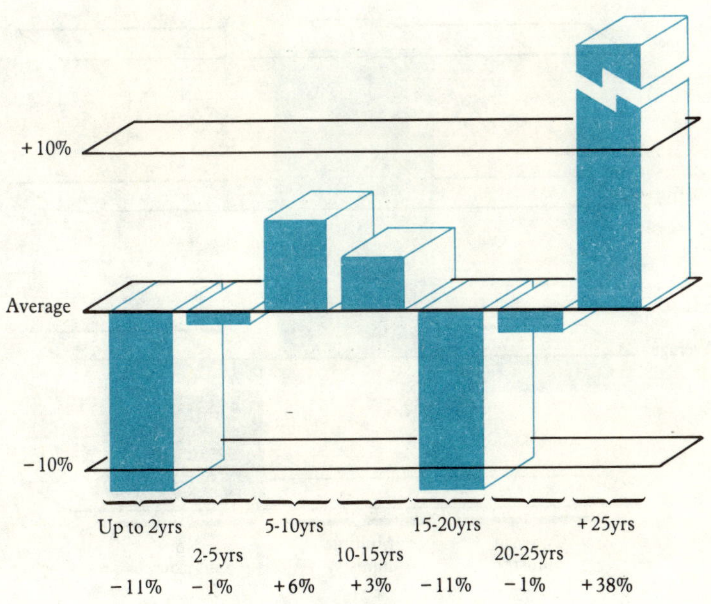

Fig. 9   Length of service in present church

33

Of greater significance was the question relating to length of service within one church. Wagner has written, 'Pastors of growing churches are generally characterized by longevity in the ministry.' By this he means long serving within the one church. This was confirmed in our survey. It is not until a minister has served for 5 to 10 years in his church that a bias towards growth becomes evident. In other words, it takes time for fruit to emerge from someone's leadership. This finding has significantly altered my own approach to the ministry at Altrincham. Initially I had seen myself as ministering for a relatively short period of time, particularly as it is my first pastorate.

Then there is the question of multiple ministry. About two-thirds of all Baptist ministers operate on their own: in our sample, 225 churches out of 327 were in this position. However, in the remaining 102 churches, there were 46 cases where specific pastoral assistance of various kinds had been provided. This took a variety of forms, from that of

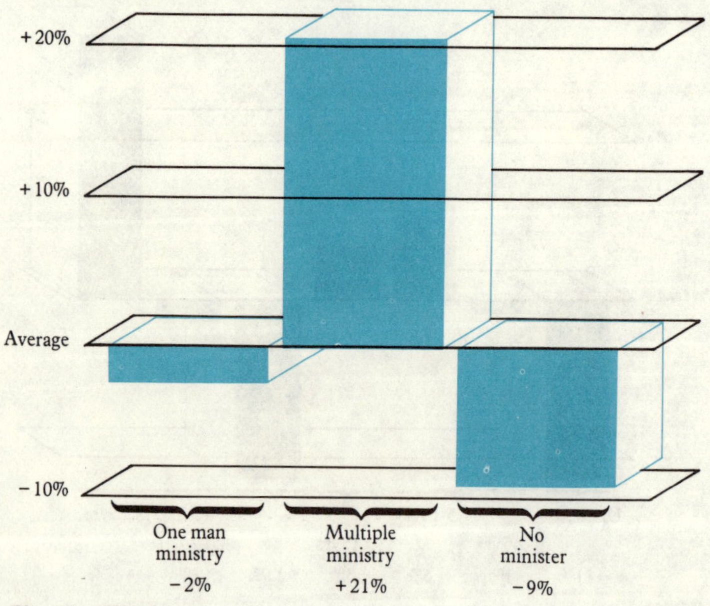

Fig. 10   Number of ministers

full-time assistant to a part-time helper, or even some combination of the two. The important point is that where any type of multiple ministry is present there is a very definite bias towards growth.

This statistic needs to be interpreted with caution. (Fig. 10) Does the growth result from having more full or part-time ministers? Or does the extra ministerial help come as a result of the growth? It is the chicken and the egg problem all over again.

Positive Leadership
Peter Wagner stresses the positive leadership qualities of a minister. Leadership, vision and possibility-thinking all represent the key gifts of the pastor in a growing church. Our research took this up by looking at four characteristics of a minister.

In the questionnaire we asked church officers to list in order of priority the particular strengths of their minister. Was his forte preaching, pastoral care, administration, or vision/leadership? As might be expected, most churches

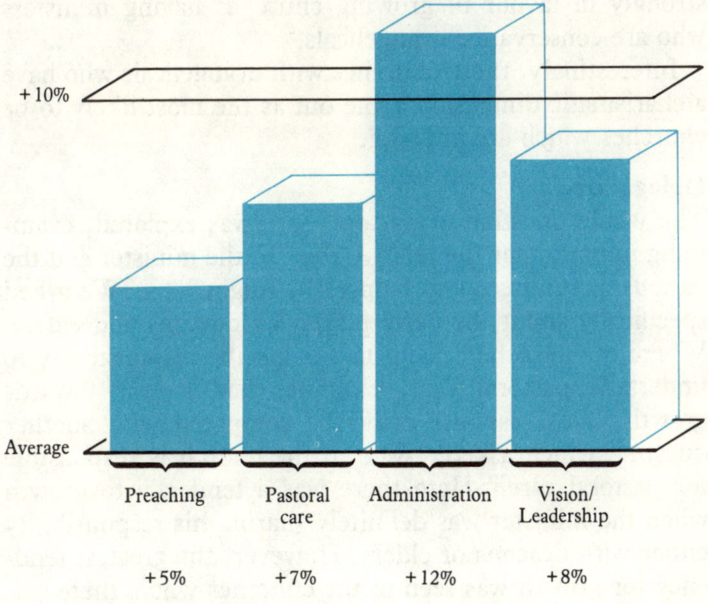

Fig. 11   Gifts of minister

thought their minister was a good preacher and pastor. However, there was a bias in favour of churches growing where administration and leadership/vision were recognized as the prime gifts. (Fig. 11)

Theology
The Church Growth Movement has surfaced within the evangelical stream of the Christian Church. Certainly in America it is the evangelical churches which are growing. For Wagner it is clearly essential for a Church Growth pastor to hold an evangelical position. Not that holding the correct doctrine in itself is enough. As Wagner writes, 'If a church declares that saving souls is its top priority but violates a half dozen of the Church Growth principles, it cannot expect to grow.'

With this in mind we asked churches to list their minister's theological position, even though we recognize that people cannot be as neatly and precisely categorized as statisticians, and particularly computers, may desire. Perhaps not surprisingly, this analysis (Fig. 12) showed strongly in favour of growing churches having ministers who are conservative evangelicals.

Interestingly, those churches with evangelicals who have a charismatic dimension come out as the most likely to be churches which are growing.

Delegation
The whole question of pastoral care was explored, examining in particular the relative roles of the minister and the various committees and helpers he might have. We asked specifically about the parts played by deacons and elders. Where one or other group had a specific responsibility to undertake pastoral care, churches had a bias towards growth. This response could be compared with another question which asked, 'Who in the church is responsible for pastoral care?' Here there was a tendency to growth when the minister was definitely sharing his responsibility either with deacons or elders. However, the greatest tendency for growth was seen in the churches where there was

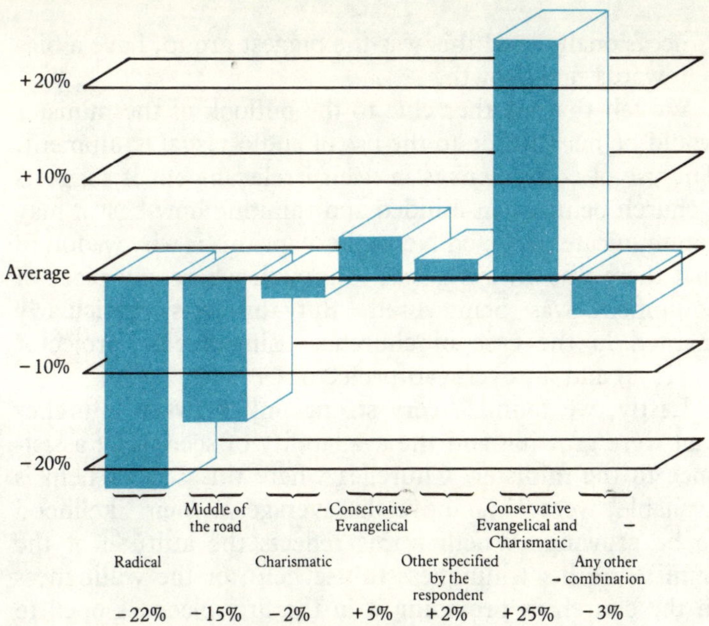

Fig. 12   Theological position of minister

a specific pastoral care team. From this we concluded that a minister's capability for leadership was reflected in his ability to delegate pastoral responsibilities. If a church is to grow, the minister must share the pastoral work.

A further way to evaluate the attitude of the minister in terms of Peter Wagner's assertion was to look at the Sunday Services. These would be a guide to his attitude. We discovered that there was a significant bias towards growth in the churches

- which had frequent participation by lay members in the services (+ 7%), particularly when this involved witness (+ 13%), and preaching (+ 11%).
- which had guest services quarterly (+ 5%) or occasionally (+ 8%).
- where the minister made appeals following baptisms (+ 9%) or even more frequently than that (+ 27%).
- where outreach services were planned weekly (+ 28%). However, those churches that only hold such services

occasionally, and this was the biggest group, have a bias towards non-growth.

We felt that another clue to the outlook of the minister would be his attitude to the use of audio-visual equipment. The use of equipment is in itself irrelevant but it suggests a church being open-minded and thinking how best it may communicate the Good News. Perhaps this is why we found that there was always a bias to growth where any piece of equipment was being used. But this was particularly marked in the case of churches using a cine projector (+ 15%) and an overhead projector (+ 30%).

Lastly, we found a very strong link between churches that were growing and the availability of secretarial assistance to the minister. Churches where this sort of help is available, were 13% above the average in their likelihood to be growing. Whether this reflects the attitude of the minister in his willingness to use help, or the willingness of the church in providing it in the first place, is open to discussion. However, undeniably, it frees the minister to do the sort of work he alone is able to do.

It would seem that these findings broadly support Wagner's premise that the pastor should be a possibility-thinker and a dynamic leader for growth, though it is perhaps more important that he should have a willingness or ability to delegate or share his responsibilities with the members in his fellowship. There is a fruitful interdependence which neither party can achieve on its own. This is something on which I will comment later.

ARE THE LAITY MOBILIZED?
The second of Peter Wagner's Signs of a growing church is that it will have 'a well-mobilized laity which has discovered, developed and is using all the spiritual gifts for growth.'

Part of the truth of this statement has already been seen in the previous section, where churches with a team of lay members involved in pastoral care have a tendency for growth. This demonstrates the commitment of the laity who are using this spiritual gift. There was also reference to the bias for growth when lay members participated regularly in church services. Again this indicated a mobilized laity.

There are a number of activities in church life such as Bible study, prayer, welcoming of new members to the fellowship, evangelism and other similarly related matters which depend on lay participation and leadership. So we looked at these.

We found that churches with prayer groups – and thus a good level of lay leaders – clearly had bias to growth. (Fig. 13)

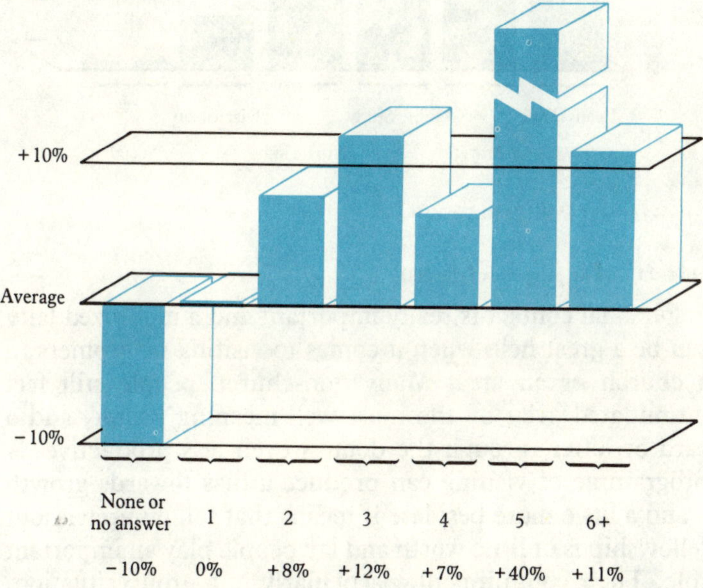

Fig. 13   Number of prayer groups

Small cell groups also revealed a similar movement, particularly when their prime objective was evangelism. These data show that prayer cells are likely to be more productive in Church Growth than Bible study cells. This is not surprising, in that it surely indicates a greater involvement of the lay members. Prayer groups presuppose active participation. In contrast, it is possible to be part of a Bible study

group and still not be any more than intellectually interested. (Fig. 14)

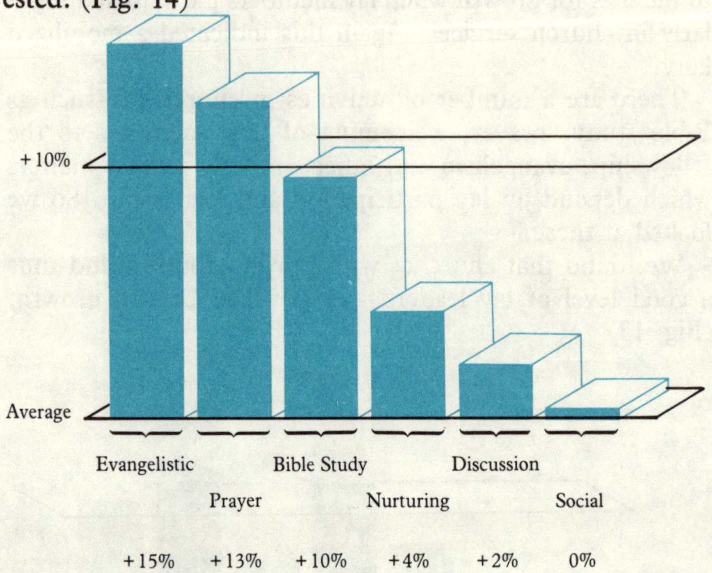

Fig. 14   The purpose of the cell

Personal contact is really important and a mobilized laity
can be a great help when it comes to visiting newcomers to
a church or an area. Many non-church people still feel
intimidated even by the most well-meaning pastor, and a
card or letter through the door is even less productive. A
programme of visiting can produce a bias towards growth
– and a little more besides. It means that follow-up without
fellowship is of little worth and lay people play an important
role. Their commitment, particularly in a group situation,
can be most productive of growth. On the other hand, our
research has shown that it is the churches which do not
make any provision for nurturing which have the least
tendency towards growth.

There have been recent changes in the whole field of
pastoral care and the survey examined the effect these had
had over the last five years. Where lay people had been
included in this sort of work there was a marked bias

towards growth (+ 22%). There were further positive signs when the different levels of participation were studied. As more lay people became involved, and so permitted more sharing of the load, a growth figure of + 18% was recorded; and where more prayer and Bible study groups had sprung up, the bias towards growth was + 20%. Also showing a strong bias towards growth were churches who said that over the past five years they had received an influx in able lay people who could assist with pastoral care (+ 29%).

Another aspect that demonstrates the mobilization of lay members is their involvement with outreach. But this is best considered under a later section of this survey.

The survey makes it clear that a committed laity is a vital factor in Church Growth, both in terms of the numbers being reached and the quality of lives of the members themselves. When the members of the congregation are spiritually alive, a minister with vision can take them on to great things. When they are spiritually lethargic, they can frustrate the very best leader. So it is important when considering a programme for growing a church that there is an honest and realistic appraisal of the real strength of the members. It may be that the first step would have to be the deepening of the faith and general spiritual life of a small group of the members who would then become catalysts in the whole reaction.

IS THE CHURCH BIG ENOUGH TO COPE?
The third proposition by Wagner is that a growing church needs to be 'big enough to provide a range of services that meets the needs and expectation of its members.' Our survey is ill-equipped to evaluate this Vital Sign, for the very way in which we chose our sample churches eliminated those congregations which were too small. However, one of the aspects of Wagner's 'big enough' concept is that a church should be able to provide a full range of activities in order to meet the needs of each member of a family. This is logical in that a church needs to make itself attrac-

41

tive to the new people coming into close contact with it for the first time.

Nevertheless, there was one aspect of our analysis which calls into question the accuracy of this Vital Sign, at least so far as English churches are concerned. We spent some time trying to correlate the number of people that each church had won for Christ over the past five years with the different levels of activity that the church perceived to have an evangelistic purpose. We could find no correlation whatsoever; nor could we discover any relationship between the total activity in the church and the number of those being converted.

It was staggering to discover the sheer volume of activities undertaken by some churches – youth organizations, women's groups, men's fellowships and so on – where the number of conversions over the past five years had been virtually nil. It is not wrong to provide social services for the community, but to do so under the misconception that they are serving an evangelistic end is only to fool ourselves.

It is true that such a wide spread of activities may have a long-term effect. Yet there did not seem to be any evidence from the survey that this could actually be measured in terms of conversions. So it seems debatable whether the high level of activities in so many churches can be justified on the grounds of contributing to spiritual growth.

Thus while we are conscious of the need to cater for all ages in the fellowship, for all members of a family, it would seem a positive advantage for the activities to be spiritually based rather than for them to be secular in the belief that they will be attractive and will keep people in contact with the church. This does not mean that the physical resources of the church should not be used for purely social purposes. But care should be taken not to dissipate resources, particularly in terms of the people whose gifts could also be deployed to spiritual ends.

WHAT IS THE TRUTH ABOUT CELEBRATIONS,
CONGREGATIONS AND CELLS?

Peter Wagner's fourth Vital Sign is that the local church should be able to provide its members with involvement in three different kinds of relationship based on the size and purpose of the group gathered together. These three are what he defines as *celebration*, *congregation* and *cell*. He sees the presence of all three as essential in a church which is growing. He defines the terms as follows:

Celebration

This is a corporate act of worship which, according to Wagner, first and foremost involves *celebration*. By that he means something more than worship, which can equally be a solitary experience. Celebration should be the main function of Sunday services and in our survey we have identified the *celebration* activity with Sunday congregations.

Congregation

This is best described as *a fellowship circle* or *fellowship group* – a peer group where each person knows all the others by name. Such groups take a variety of forms but the need which they meet, whether consciously or not, is that of social fellowship. In the survey, the term *congregation* has been applied to all regular church-based meetings, such as Sunday School or a mid-week Women's Fellowship.

Cell

This is a *spiritual kinship group* – a group of around 8 to 12 people who, though meeting for prayer and Bible study, have as their main function, close personal fellowship. The survey applies the term *cell* to small groups generally with an avowed spiritual purpose (house groups, fellowship groups, Bible study and prayer groups).

Church

The difficulty in relating this *celebration* + *congregation* + *cell* = *church* concept to the survey is that the terms do not all readily transfer into a British context. For Wagner the optimum size of a congregation is 120, which relates closely to a British equivalent of what we have taken to be a celebration. In fact, there can be very few British churches large enough to contain more than two congregations within their Sunday celebratory group.

It is worth noting, however, that many American churches also have this problem, despite the influence of Church Growth thinking. Eight out of ten American churches have a Sunday attendance of 200 or less. If this 200 barrier is to be broken then the idea of fellowship groups has to be developed. As Wagner says, 'If a church makes the multiplication of congregation or fellowship groups a definite part of its planning for growth, the Church will almost inevitably grow faster.'

When Wagner talks about celebration, he has in mind the result of a lot of people coming together, hungry to meet God. On such an occasion a special kind of worship can take place. Sociologists recognize that certain laws of human behaviour operate differently in large and small groups. The same sporting event somehow seems more

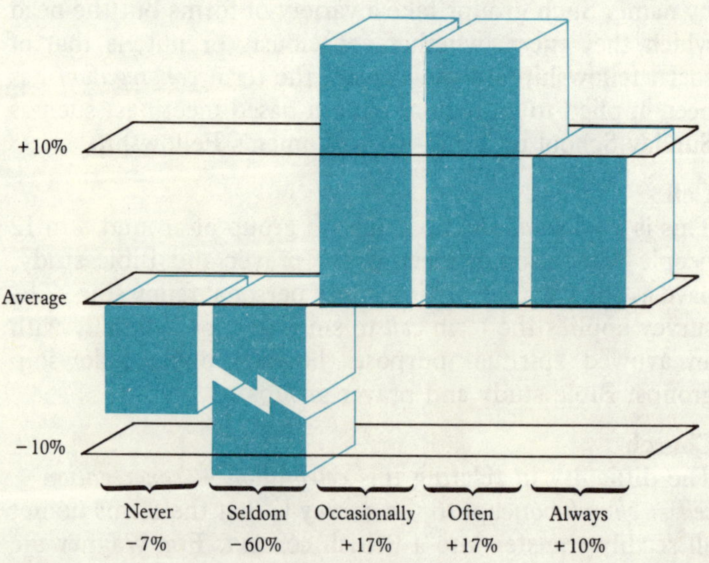

Fig. 15   **Music other than piano and organ**

exciting when it takes place in a packed stadium rather than in a deserted field. What is needed, Wagner says, is a Sunday gathering of celebration which has people heading for their Sunday dinner feeling they have just had an important meeting with God and because of it they are not the same.

Our survey had no way to judge which churches sent their people home on Sundays feeling like that, although experience tells us that there may not be many! However, there was one aspect in the survey that linked to the concept of worship being a celebration event. There was a question asked on how often music other than piano or organ was used. Fig. 15 shows the result.

Initially there were problems in relating the survey to the activities of celebration and congregation, though we were able to measure the level of cell activity. Eventually we asked churches to list all their church activities and give the frequency of each, together with the average attendance. From this it was possible to determine the number

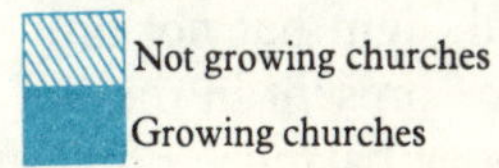

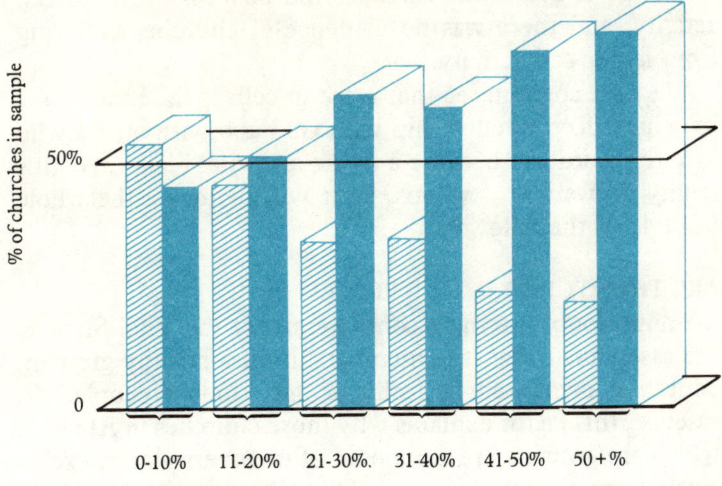

Fig. 16   Cell activity as % of total activity

of people attending each activity in a month. From here we could break the activities down under the three headings of celebration, congregation and cell. As a result, we could discover the total number of bodies involved under each heading in each month.

It was revealing to tabulate the percentage of cell activities in both the growing and non-growing churches. (Fig. 16) We discovered that as the percentage of cell activity increases in the total programme so does the probability that a church is a growing one.

Closer investigation of the churches which were growing over the ten years with acceleration (Trend 5, page 24, figure 2) revealed that more than two-thirds of them had at least a quarter of their activity in cell groups.

In contrast, a church that was not growing was less likely to have a good proportion of cell activity. The churches which had been more or less static over 10 years and those actually declining had more than 7 out of 10 of their number spending less than a quarter of their time in cell groups.

The survey supported Wagner's Vital Sign that not only should all these three types of activity be present in the life of a church but there should be a proper balance. For us this came to mean that there should be a high level of cell activity, and there was no evidence of churches suffering from hyper-cell activity.

We have come to see that work in cells is the best means by which deeper fellowship with God and with others who love the Lord can become a living and vital reality. As this reality grows and develops, so it will permeate the whole lifestyle of the fellowship.

ARE THEY YOUR KIND OF PEOPLE?

Without doubt the most controversial of the Vital Signs is the assessment that 'the membership of a healthy growing church is composed basically of one kind of people.' In essence, this factor explains why those churches in America which are growing are composed of members almost exclusively from one ethnic group. The fact that different ethnic groups exist is hardly surprising seeing that more than one American citizen in five reports that some tongue other than English is his mother tongue.

But *the one kind of people*, in Church Growth jargon 'a homogeneous unit', relates not only to ethnic factors but also to cultural ones. A growing church, says Wagner, is more likely to have its members predominantly drawn from one social class. This can be reflected in terms of housing – private or council; occupation – manual or clerical; and so on. It is a matter of like attracting like.

In some parts of this country, particularly the South of England, there are large neighbourhoods that are clearly defined. There are the 'gin and jag' areas and the 'beer and bike' areas. And whatever we may feel about the homogeneous principle in church life it can be seen in many situations. Crusader classes for example were almost exclusively based on one segment of society.

While we may have an intuitive feeling that like will attract like in bringing a person to the point of conversion, we also have a natural resistance to the notion that Christians of different backgrounds cannot worship and work together. Nevertheless, one factor in motivating this survey was my own experience at Altrincham where we could see this beginning to be the situation in our fellowship and yet we were powerless to do anything about it.

No reliable evidence on this Vital Sign was forthcoming from our survey since very few of the churches who replied had more than a few per cent of new commonwealth immigrants in their congregation or were in areas which were highly mixed racially. However, where the survey provided data that could indicate homogeneity in terms of housing, employment and education, these tended *not* to support the homogeneous principle. Many fellowships were thoroughly mixed and closely reflected the variety in their immediate environment.

ARE THE METHODS KNOWN TO WORK?
The sixth Vital Sign that Peter Wagner had observed was
that a growing church 'is using evangelistic methods which
are known to work'. With this in mind, the questionnaire
opened up the way to investigate several areas relating
specifically to evangelism.

It came as no surprise to find that the more evangelistic
activities undertaken by a church, the greater is the probability that the church is growing. (Fig. 17)

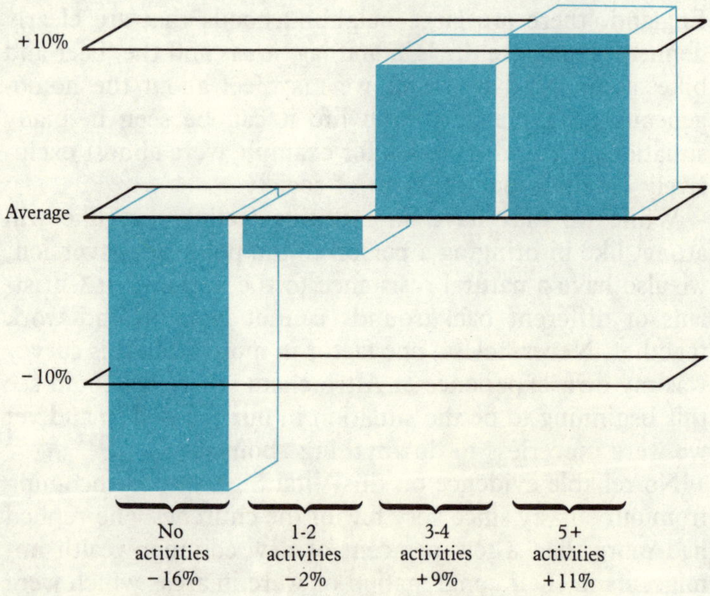

Fig. 17   Activities in outreach

Churches with a specific committee responsible for outreach are more likely to be growing. This was contrary to
the experience of those who suggested the question and
who saw such a committee as the last desperate throw of
a dying church. There was an even higher probability
among those churches with a specific evangelistic programme. (Fig. 18)

48

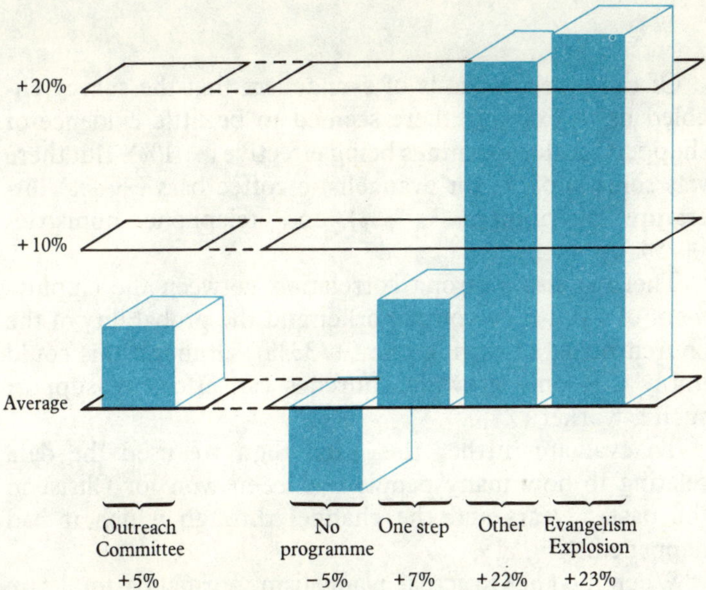

Fig. 18   Type of evangelistic activity

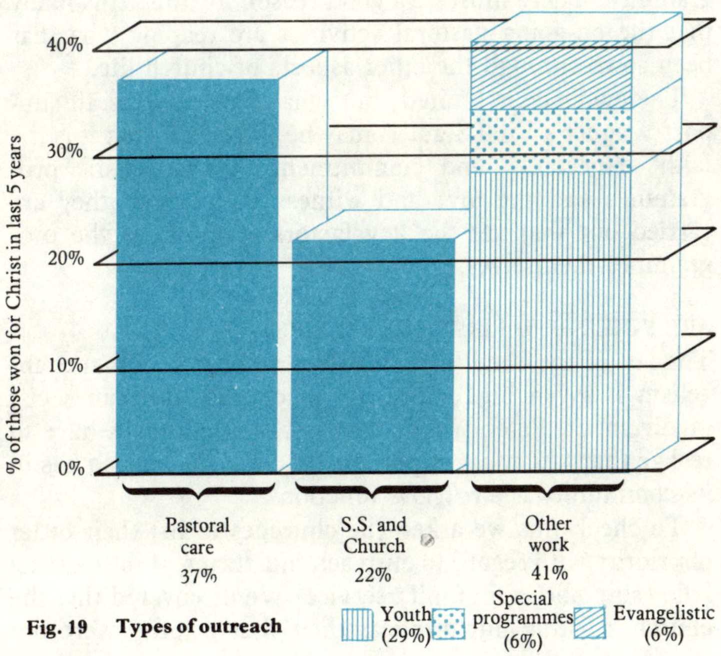

Fig. 19   Types of outreach

Of the other methods of evangelism that the survey enabled us to examine there seemed to be little evidence of shoppers' coffee mornings being effective (− 1%). But there was some support for evangelistic coffee bars (+ 4%), literature distribution (+ 3%) and telephone ministries (+ 5%).

There is also a strong correlation between the employment of a full-time youth worker and the probability of the church being a growing one (+ 33%), although this could imply that only growing churches can afford to support such a worker.

To evaluate further this Vital Sign we used the data relating to how many people had been won for Christ in the past 5 years and the channel through which it had happened. (Fig. 19)

When it comes to actual evangelism, normal pastoral care appears to be more effective than Sunday School, youth work, special missions, or even so-called evangelistic programmes. There must be a good reason for this. It is likely that the on-going pastoral activities are reaping what has been sown through the other aspects of church life.

The evidence is limited, but what there is does all support Wagner's Vital Sign. It may be, however, that it is the faith, expectancy and commitment to evangelistic programmes and the love and witness with which they are carried out that are the key factors as much as the programmes themselves.

ARE YOU DOING FIRST THINGS FIRST?

The last of the Vital Signs involves making sure that evangelism is given higher priority in church life than social involvement. Peter Wagner stresses that churches have to realize that 'the most important function the church has in its community is a *religious* function'.

To check this we asked the churches to list their order of priority with regard to outreach, nurturing of the existing fellowship and community service. We discovered that the churches listing nurturing as their first priority were not more likely to be growing than the average. But those churches that listed outreach as either their first or second priority had a strong bias towards growth.

Meanwhile, those churches who considered that community service was their main task had a definite bias towards non-growth.

Once again, placing outreach in first or second ranking may reflect awareness and commitment to going out into the world in response to Christ's commission.

HIGH WATERMARKS

- Five of the Seven Vital Signs were broadly supported by our work in the English context. The homogeneity principle was difficult to support or refute, whilst with our present understanding of growth, we would not see size as a limitation (see next chapter for development of this together with new evidence). Other factors are much more important.
- For each and every one of the factors we analysed, there was a significant proportion – but less than the average – of churches displaying that factor who were in fact losing members.
- The sharing in some manner of the total span of ministry, and of the building up of the spiritual vitality of the members in small group work, seem to be of primary importance in making disciples. This is not to exclude the other Vital Signs.

Chapter 5

Enigma Variations

SUPERMAN OR SUPERSLOG?

Now we have all the ingredients we need to build up our own 'super-pastor', a figure guaranteed to bring success in any Church Growth scheme no matter what the situation may be. And what would this bionic miracleman be like? Well, he would be in his thirties and would have been in the ministry for five to ten years. He would have been in his present pastorate for five years and his theology would be that of a conservative evangelical with some charismatic overtones. The music he would choose for worship would be accompanied by more than the piano and organ, at least some of the time. And he would be a dab hand at using an overhead projector.

If only it were that easy!

At Altrincham Baptist Church we could see parallels with some of the essential ingredients for a church to grow. Yet numerical growth within the church was slowing down. Sifting through the piles of computer data and completed questionnaires, Alan and I began to see that there were two major factors that related to our own situation and, no doubt, they were affecting other churches as well.

We noticed that although a number of the churches were

doing many of the things that Peter Wagner said were essential, they were still not growing (see chapter 4). That even included the church that had the largest number of small groups in action of any fellowship in the survey. And conversely, some of the churches who were apparently doing everything wrong were actually in League Division 1 of the growth tables. These enigmas demanded closer inspection.

Alan's long sessions in pre-coding the survey forms ready for the computer had been eased slightly by a little game he played as he worked. The first five pages of the questionnaire described the environment of the church and its activities. By this stage he could gauge whether or not that particular church was actually growing. He worked this out from the quality – often indefinable – of certain answers and also the balance of activities. Before long, he was getting the answer right nearly every time, though the truth was not revealed until the thirteenth or fourteenth page. He recalls one church though, where the first section of the form could be little more than a forecast of doom and disaster. Everything about it seemed to be wrong and Alan had made up his mind that it must be on its very last legs. Yet he reached the statistics section of the questionnaire to find that the opposite was true. The church was growing like wildfire.

We set out to discover why and came to the conclusion the growth was almost entirely due to people transferring from other churches to this one. The fellowship was situated in a geographical area of high mobility in terms of housing and population. It was the one church in the area and, due to social conditions, was reaping what it very definitely had not sown.

HOW DOES YOUR CHURCH GROW?
Obviously, there are three distinct ways in which a church can grow numerically. American Church Growth protagonists have always held these in view. They are, namely, biological growth, transfer growth and conversion growth.

54

Biological growth takes place through Christians bringing their children up in the faith – something which, incidentally, Peter Wagner considers should automatically account for a church growing by 25% every 10 years!

Transfer growth is when people move from one area to another, as a result of local development, new jobs, housing, industrialization, and so on.

Conversion growth adds to a church through people being won over to Jesus Christ.

In spite of these three aspects being recognized by the Church Growth Movement, the concept of transfer growth has been almost completely ignored. Not one of Peter Wagner's Seven Vital Signs pauses to ask the question as to where any resulting growth has come from. Consequently, transfer growth may look impressive on a church's statistical record, but in national terms it is of no significance at all. It is rather like taking money from your left pocket and putting it into your right one. You are not one penny richer as a result!

Transfer growth can often be a smoke screen which obscures the real situation. Unless the factors associated with it are carefully evaluated, churches can be open to some serious self-deception. There will be some congregations living in Cloud Cuckoo Land, energetically patting themselves on the back as their congregation expands. Yet they may be dealing with a predominantly transfer growth situation and not growing at all in real terms. Meanwhile, there will be other fellowships suffering from a severe lack of confidence in the face of constant numerical decline resulting from a population exodus which exceeds the fruits of their hard work in conversion.

Yet it must be said that not all transfer growth can be explained away by the natural movement of an area's inhabitants. There can be other causes which are destructive. For example, we became aware of one Baptist church whose dynamic growth had clearly been at the expense of another Baptist fellowship nearby. Transfer growth can be like Robin Hood in reverse. It robs the poor in order to give to the rich. Almost the whole membership of one had been attracted to the other as a result of the dynamic preaching and teaching of one man. But what will happen when that man finally moves on? This church could be building on sand.

There is strong evidence in the survey that the churches which are growing in numbers also attract members to themselves by means of transfer. And these newcomers are often the most able and committed people from other churches. So the growth is at the expense of other fellowships actually in the same neighbourhood.

This destructive aspect of transfer growth was made evident by answers to one of the questions. We asked the churches who reported having more people now assisting with pastoral care than there had been five years earlier to identify where these increased resources had come from. The majority spoke of the responsibility being taken by new people who had come into the fellowship from outside. This meant that their improvement had been at the expense of other churches, rather than through the development of the existing members.

This was the first of the two major factors we discovered that particularly reflected upon our own situation in Altrincham and one to which we gave close attention. From a human perspective it is obviously understandable that growing churches will attract spiritually lively people and divert gifted individuals away from the less fortunate neighbouring fellowships. Every time this happens the gap between weak and strong neighbouring churches grows even larger.

However, there is also a positive aspect to transfer growth. It can provide a major lifeline to what would otherwise be a seemingly hopeless situation.

We have already seen the relevance of Peter Wagner's Vital Sign relating to the essential role of lay leadership in the church. But supposing the minister is bereft of people capable of sharing the leadership with him? One hope is that the church will eventually attract those with whom he can share the leadership, or he has to develop that first catalytic group.

WHEN BIGGER ISN'T BETTER

A second major clue to our situation at Altrincham came from the results in the survey showing the growth and non-growth profile of churches with various sizes of membership. This data brought us to the inescapable conclusion that the size of a church had some bearing on the likelihood of it being a growing fellowship.

Two distinct bands of membership size have a consistent bias towards growth, while two other bands have a bias towards the likelihood of them not being growing churches.

The questions that these facts raised are obvious:

- Why is it that a church with a membership between 100 and 150 members is more likely to be a growing one than a fellowship with 100 or less members?
- Why is a church less likely to be a growing one when it breaks through the 150 member barrier?
- Why did the likelihood of growth return when a church had more than 300 members? (Fig. 6 see page 28)

Satisfactory answers to these questions could not be found by comparing the activities of the churches within the various size bands. The on-going programmes of many of them were remarkably similar. Yet there was this great disparity in the likelihood of fellowships of different sizes being growing ones. Instead, it seems clear that the governing factor is the role played by the minister himself.

What I could see was the effect of the limitations of a one-man ministry operation. A full-time pastor could cope with the demands of a growing church with a membership under 150. But beyond that point, the strain and limitations begin to have an adverse effect on the potential for growth of the church. Interestingly, this is confirmed by the valuable work of David Wasdell of the Urban Growth Unit. His studies indicate that one man's ministry is limited to caring for a congregation of about 175. Beyond that point it is essential that there should be extra assistance for him.

This may be full or part-time help; it may be provided through an additional minister; or by training lay members to take further responsibility.

So it was in Altrincham and as our church approached the 150 mark and the growth process began to slow down, I became involved in the issues of church growth. Our experience had finally exposed my own limitations in trying to contain all the pastoral needs of the fellowship. I had been trying to cope physically, intellectually and sociologically with an ever-widening range of activities. I felt like the circus juggler with an ever-growing row of spinning plates on bamboo poles. As each new plate is added, there is the danger that the other plates will crash down behind him.

But things change when a church moves into the 300 member bracket. It is likely that at around this point a fellowship finally concedes that a traditional one-man ministry approach is not enough. The congregation is forced either to appoint extra ministers or assistants, or to share the pastoral and leadership roles among its senior members. Where this happens the church growth brakes are off and the future looks good once again.

The survey had not only put Peter Wagner's Seven Vital Signs well and truly to the test. It had also provided a definite indication of the factors which were hindering the continued growth of Altrincham. Now it was time for action. This voyage of exploration had never been simply an academic exercise. We had to lay out a plan of action based on all we had learnt.

HIGH WATERMARKS
- Transfer growth is both a blessing and a danger. It is the most common means by which spiritually catalytic people come into a fellowship, but over-concentration can denude other churches in a variety of ways which can be quite damaging.
- The bigger the church the greater the need for a sharing of the total ministry.

- There are almost certainly limitations to a one-man ministry regardless of the size of the fellowship.

Chapter 6

Spiral bound

THE WAY AHEAD

Four main factors governed my thinking as I mapped out the way ahead for the church, based on the findings of the survey. Firstly, it was clear that some of the Vital Signs shown by growing churches were also present in non-growing churches. The survey made it clear that the simple application of the Seven Vital Signs does not necessarily ensure growth.

Secondly, much of the growth that was evident was not real growth at all. It actually related to people who were transferring in from other churches. The fact that a church was growing did not necessarily mean that the church was being successful in terms of winning outsiders for Christ. Many 'growing' churches in our survey were reporting that few actual conversions were taking place. On average the survey revealed only 16 conversions in each growing church over the past five years – just over three conversions per year. When you remember that all the churches in the survey had a membership of fifty or more, the average being 132, three per year is not a very spectacular figure, even though we were dealing with averages covering a wide spread of individual figures.

A third factor facing me was that growing churches tended to depend for any improved leadership or pastoral care on new people transferring in from other churches. In many cases numerical growth seemed to have little to do with the personal growth and development of the existing members. Yet, if we understand the Great Commission correctly, disciple-making does not end with conversion. Disciples are to be taught to obey all that Jesus has commanded, which involves the winning of others.

Finally, there were the limitations relating to a one-man ministry. Churches with a membership of more than 150 were less likely to be growing. This seemed to indicate a limit to the number of people with which one man could cope.

It was while we were wrestling with these factors and looking for ways to relate them to the day-to-day life at Altrincham that Alan had a sudden flash of inspiration. It proved to be of major importance in the development of our thinking, bringing into focus what had gone before.

We had been trying to define the role of a local church by listing its responsibilities. In doing so we had hoped to discover areas which we were not covering in Altrincham. By defining the full role or mission of the church we hoped to ensure that we tackled every aspect for which we were responsible, rather than majoring on some and neglecting others.

EUREKA!
But definitions only take you part of the way. We needed to go further and indeed it took an actual journey to put us on the right road. It happened like this: Alan and I were on our way south on the M1, bound for London Bible College and the first consultation on Church Growth ever to take place in Britain. We were heading for something else too – our own eureka moment, an experience such as Alan had had years ago when working in the laboratory. He had been puzzling over a particularly difficult problem when a chance remark of a colleague during the tea break

cracked the whole thing open. All he had to do was to write out the formulae and then put them into practice.

Well, now we needed our own particular formula. Alan already had some ideas when we stopped for coffee at a motorway service station. Things had begun to move. But it was at the conference that they really speeded up. We were going to London to share some of the preliminary findings of our survey. This was to happen in the afternoon, so in the morning we each attended a separate study group. In his, Alan overheard something which started his brain racing.

A minister in the group said, 'I feel I have a very good teaching ministry'. It wasn't what he said but how he said it. The tone struck a chord in Alan's mind. When the Production Director of a commercial company boasts in that self-satisfied sort of voice, 'We have a very good production system in this organization', the warning lights begin to flash. Something is wrong somewhere. One side of the operation is taking over and that can be dangerous.

In nature, a balance has to be kept. If there are too many greenfly, watch out for ladybirds. And big business – and the Church too – can learn from nature. Alan knew this. Once the balance is upset disaster can strike. So an organization has to make sure that no single one of its functions dominates at the expense of the others.

So the tone in which the minister spoke of his preaching ability set off Alan's own private alarm. To his very practical mind, the parallels with the business world were all too obvious. He began to think what would be done by a company whose strength and abilities lay in only one direction.

A small company may be forced to accept an inherent weakness during its early stages. But failure to correct the situation as soon as possible would leave it vulnerable in the extreme. Thus Alan could see that for a church to be dependent upon one man, whatever his gifts, was equally as dangerous as a business company being dependent upon one person or one area of specialization.

A dynamic and growing business enterprise demands a well-chosen team, each member complementing the others. If the founder of the company is an extrovert salesman, then he needs to be complemented by a slower and more solid stay-at-home type, able to control operations with care and thoroughness. There has to be balance between the personal attributes of the staff, and the work has to be shared to take advantage of that balance. The head has to become the co-ordinator rather than the action man (1 Corinthians 12).

As we drove away from that consultation at the London Bible College, Alan told me what he had been thinking. Immediately we could see the relevance of our earlier ideas and how to modify them. So, as we returned north, Alan and I re-worked our definition of the church's role and wrote down our conclusions. The results have remained substantially unaltered since that time.

We had already begun to realize that all the activities of the church related to an on-going cyclical process. We could perceive that members went out into the world to attract people to the church, who then went on to the point where they could themselves go out into the world and win more.

We were thus concerned with the mission of a local church and were beginning to see its fulfilment and that of the Great Commission in a dynamic, spiral process. If you have ever climbed a spiral staircase in a castle turret, you will see what we mean. The stairs go on and on, upwards and forwards in a continuous sweep. Once you start climbing, you seem to become part of the movement. There are landings and branching-off places where you can change direction, but basically movement is in a steady stream in one direction. Such a picture emphasizes some important points.

- Just as a spiral is constantly on the move, so too should be a local church. A church can never be static.
- It is only possible to move round a spiral in one direction

– upwards or downwards. In the same way a church can only move in one direction.

- A spiral involves a continuous process. It cannot be broken without making it useless for ever. In Church Growth terms, if a particular section of church life is ignored for more than a short time, an inherent weakness is built into the fellowship. Some attention has to be given to everyone in the fellowship. To do this all must be arranged round the spiral's loop. This concept will be expanded later.

- Every aspect of church life is dependent upon the preceding one. For instance, to ignore teenagers for a time in order to concentrate on young marrieds might bring a momentary success. Eventually, however, there would not be any young marrieds. They would all be growing older together with no new people coming up to take their place.

There is also another way in which the 'flow' principle of the spiral relates to the function of a church. Existing Christians must be nurtured and strengthened so as to be effective in sharing their faith. If not, then few will be attracted into the fellowship and the numbers of those converted will fall, leaving the existing congregation to dwindle by simple loss, transfer or death.

These factors underline two major advantages of the spiral concept.

- It places much of the emphasis of Church Growth on the winning of new converts. Unlike much of the thinking undertaken in America, the spiral totally ignores the possibility of transfer growth. As such it becomes a genuinely British alternative to the numbers game of much of the American Church Growth thinking.

- It emphasizes the need for churches to train their members. They must develop their faith and actively share it with outsiders in a way which will attract them to the fellowship and make them want to be associated with it.

THE MISSION OF THE CHURCH

A *church* is not the building, the denomination to which it belongs, or the programme of activities in which the members participate. The Church consists of the company of people who are committed to God and to each other in seeking to see the Kingdom of God established in their locality.

The mission of the Church is:

- To do everything to God's glory and in accordance with his will as it is earnestly sought in prayer.
- To bring men and women under the rule of Christ and into the committed membership of his Church.
- To nurture new Christians and also those older in their faith – though not necessarily in the same place and at the same time – so that all may share their faith, win others for Christ and his Church, and demonstrate by their words and actions the love of God as shown in Jesus.

This is to be done:

- By the way believers live their lives – both as individuals and together with other Christians.
- By the way they share their lives in supporting and caring for one another and by responding to each other's joys and sorrows.
- By the work they do in giving their time and financial resources for the good of the local church.
- By the acts of social service they perform, not only for the fellowship but also in the community, both local and widespread.
- By their teaching and pastoral care within the fellowship.
- By their evangelism amongst those attending church and by going out into the neighbourhood.
- By the quality of their worship.

There is nothing startling in itself about this statement of mission. You will readily see it to be an extension of the Lord's Great Commission recorded in Matthew 28. The basic business of the Church is the making of disciples. This first of all involves the winning of people to Christ and his Church. It then means going on to develop them so that they in turn may go out and win others, who will go on to win others.

It is not the statement which is so significant but the way we have applied it to the ongoing life of the church.

We developed the spiral idea and produced a first model which brought out these two salient points, placing the emphasis of Church Growth on the winning of new converts, and on enabling members to develop in such a way that they in their turn, as they use their gifts, might help in attracting others to Christ. However, it did not make clear the need for a church to have a proper balance of services to all those for whom it is responsible. Thus a second model was necessary to take account of these features, and we saw that it could be done in a way that would enable a local church to measure its activities against its responsibilities.

WHYS AND WHEREFORES

To make this possible we took our statement of the role of the church and asked ourselves four separate questions. Then we fitted the answers around a series of spiral diagrams. The questions we asked were:
- For whom is the church responsible?
- What is the church *really* doing by its various activities?
- By what activities does the church attempt to meet the needs of those for whom it is responsible?
- Through whom is the church carrying out these activities?

The first question of the four is basic to the whole issue: *For whom is the church responsible?* This is the foundation on which the other three questions rest. The challenges in our mission must be worked out in terms of service to the people in contact with the church fellowship. Therefore, we placed the various stages of spiritual development in the life of an individual around the spiral (see Spiral 1).

Obviously the individuals linked into a local church fellowship will each be at a different stage of spiritual growth and the first spiral illustrates the various stages of growth into which individuals should fit. By following the sequence you can trace the progression of someone who begins by having contact with the members and activities of the church, and goes on through the various stages to become eventually someone who is influencing others to become involved.

It is possible to put any individual member of the congregation on this diagram and see what that person's next stage of growth and commitment should be. Alternatively, you can consider that the individual members of the fellowship will each be in need of every one of these activities at some time. Their needs must all be catered for, as these are the people for whom the church is responsible.

Unfortunately, it must be said that there are many Christians in churches today who are content to remain static in their spiritual lives. The concept of their making progress in order to be of service to the church and community is one they choose to ignore. One of the great challenges to any church is to tackle the task of helping these stagnant Christians to develop and to discover a sense of mission and purpose.

The next stage was to ask '*What is the church really doing by its various activities?*' (Spiral 2). Having produced the first spiral, which illustrated various stages of spiritual growth, we could then see two particular points in the cyclic process at which there is a significant interface between the Church, in the sense of the whole family of God, and the community. (See Spiral 1 again.)

Firstly there is the interaction of the committed members of the church with the uncommitted in the community at large. Or, to put it another way, at this point the church is proclaiming in word and deed its faith to the outside world. It is important to appreciate that this is the work of the entire fellowship. Witness is not something confined to those Christians who are well-established and who have developed their gifts for leadership and service. Everyone

SPIRAL 1: For whom is the church responsible?

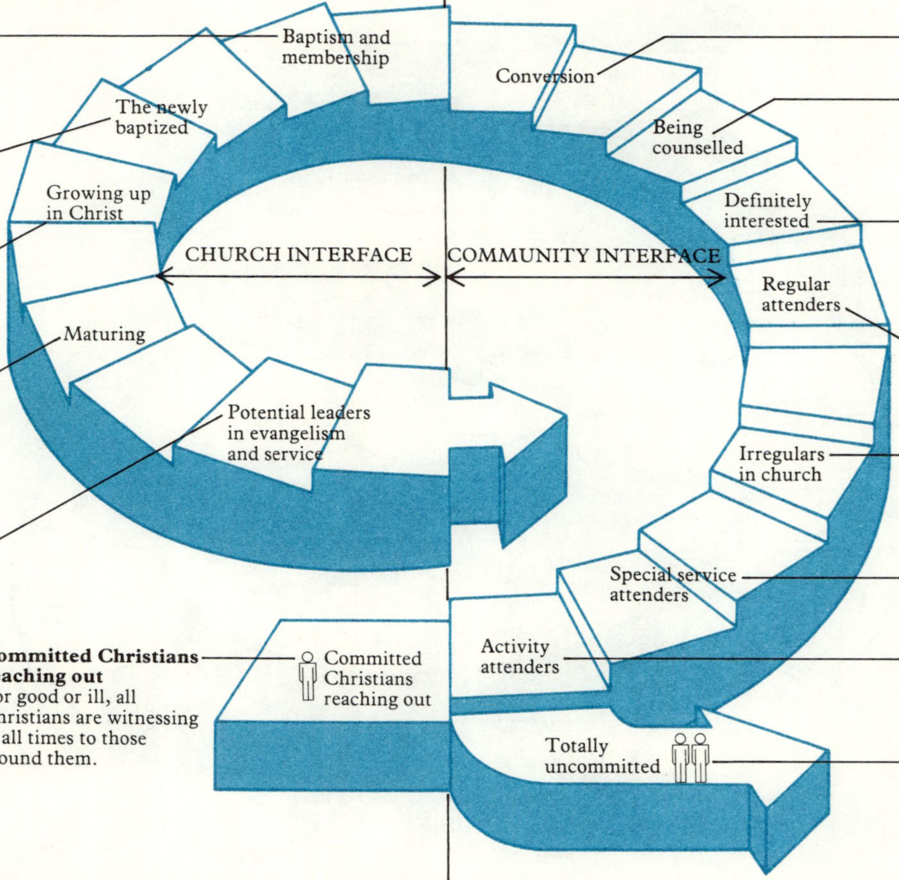

Baptism and membership
A vital step after
conversion, committing
the new Christian more
fully to Christ's family.

The newly baptized
These people are in
special need of care
and nurture.

Growing up in Christ
All in Christ's family
need continually to be
built up in faith and
understanding.

Maturing
Each Christian has at
least one spiritual gift
which has to be identified
and dedicated to God's
service.

**Potential leaders in
evangelism and service**
All members should be
helped to identify, develop
and use their gift in
the service of Christ.

**Committed Christians
reaching out**
For good or ill, all
Christians are witnessing
at all times to those
around them.

Conversion
Hallelujah!

Being counselled
Such help is usually
given on a one-to-one
basis and can lead to
commitment.

Definitely interested
Those who discover a
spiritual need and want
help in defining and
meeting it more fully.

Regular attenders
Those who find regular
attendance meets a social
or spiritual need.

Irregulars in church
Probably those who find
their social church-going
leads to a deeper interest
in Christianity.

Special service attenders
Those who come to services
at Easter, Christmas, etc.

Activity attenders
Those who come to church
for social rather than
spiritual reasons.

Totally uncommitted
Those who have contact
with church members but
have no sense of belonging
to Christ or a church.

SPIRAL 2: What is the church doing
in its various activities?

Nurturing
This is an on-going
process in which all
Christians are involved.
The needs will vary
according to the ability,
personality and spiritual
maturity of each
individual.

Developing
Every Christian has a
spiritual gift which
needs to be identified
and developed.
Training for leadership
and service is often
useful, not least that
received from assisting
more experienced members
in their jobs.

Converting
People are attracted to
services for many
different reasons. The
church's task is actively
to win them to Christ
using every means that
is appropriate.

Attracting
If Christians live
faithfully for Christ,
they will naturally
exhibit a quality which
others will admire and
desire for themselves.

Serving
Serving the needs of
one's neighbour is a
powerful witness to
Christ and may of itself
attract people to the
church. However, this
should always be a
consequence rather than
an objective of service.

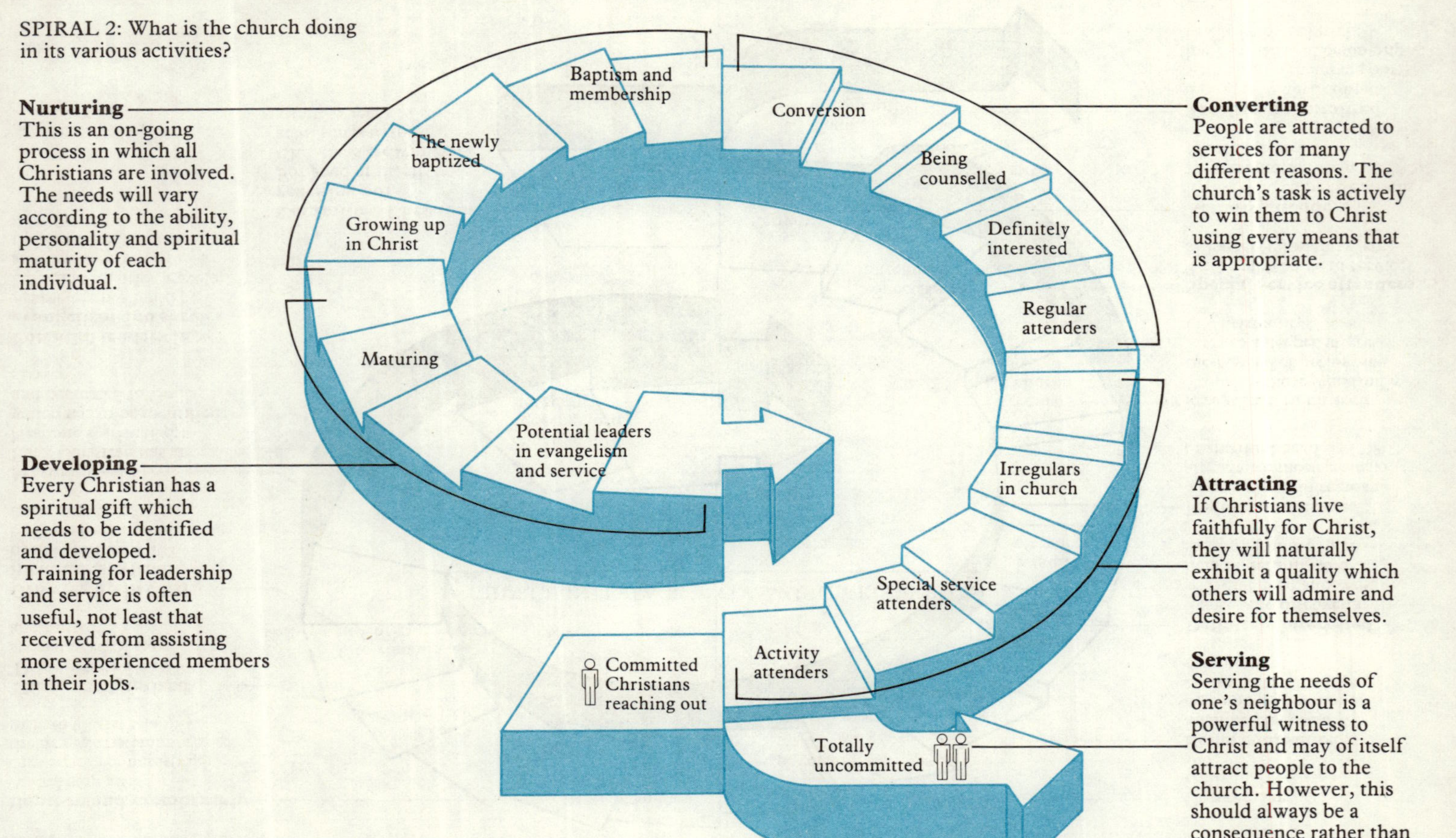

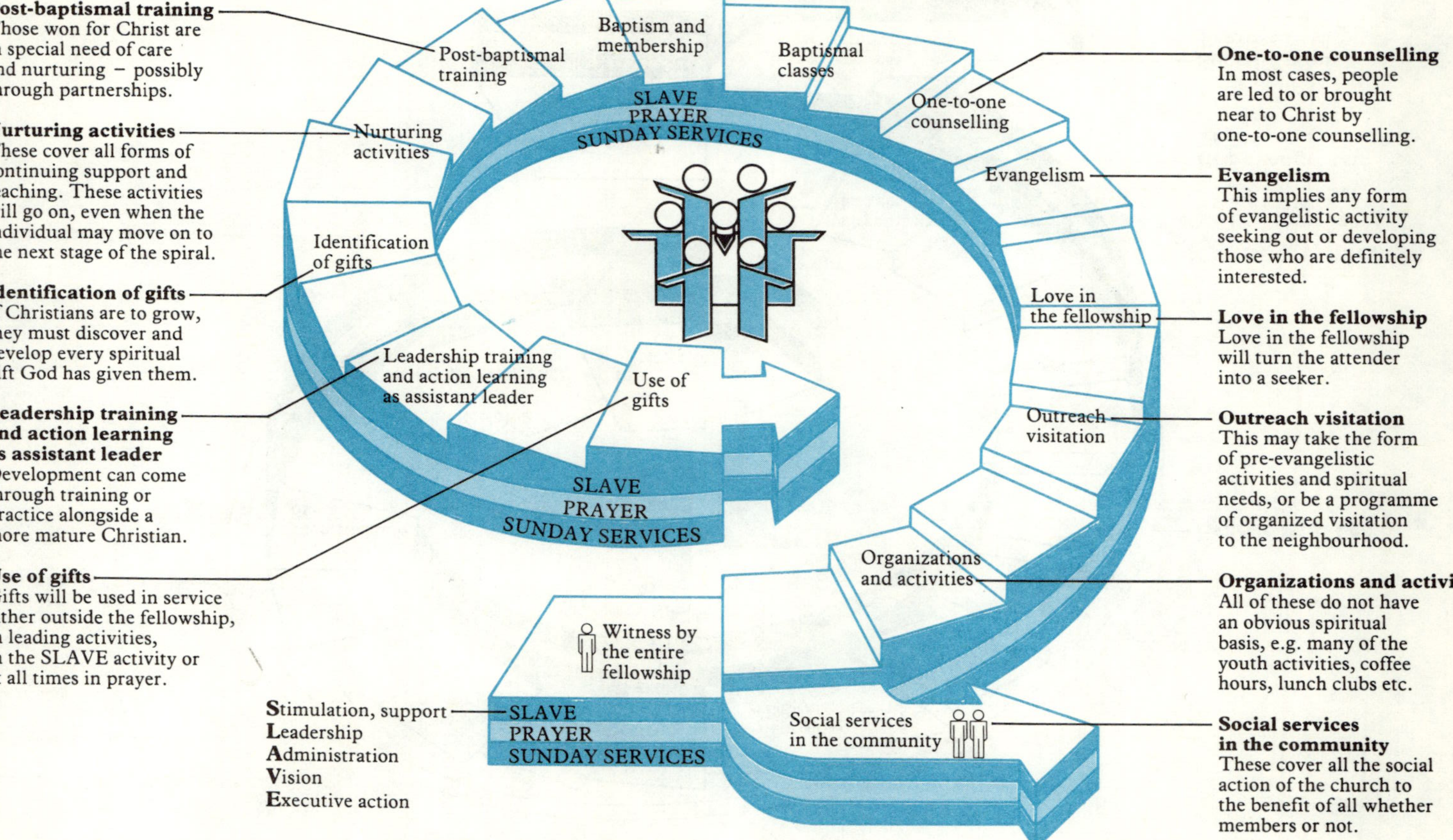

SPIRAL 3: By what activities does the church attempt to meet the needs of those for whom it is responsible?

Post-baptismal training
Those won for Christ are in special need of care and nurturing – possibly through partnerships.

Nurturing activities
These cover all forms of continuing support and teaching. These activities will go on, even when the individual may move on to the next stage of the spiral.

Identification of gifts
If Christians are to grow, they must discover and develop every spiritual gift God has given them.

Leadership training and action learning as assistant leader
Development can come through training or practice alongside a more mature Christian.

Use of gifts
Gifts will be used in service either outside the fellowship, in leading activities, in the SLAVE activity or at all times in prayer.

One-to-one counselling
In most cases, people are led to or brought near to Christ by one-to-one counselling.

Evangelism
This implies any form of evangelistic activity seeking out or developing those who are definitely interested.

Love in the fellowship
Love in the fellowship will turn the attender into a seeker.

Outreach visitation
This may take the form of pre-evangelistic activities and spiritual needs, or be a programme of organized visitation to the neighbourhood.

Organizations and activities
All of these do not have an obvious spiritual basis, e.g. many of the youth activities, coffee hours, lunch clubs etc.

Social services in the community
These cover all the social action of the church to the benefit of all whether members or not.

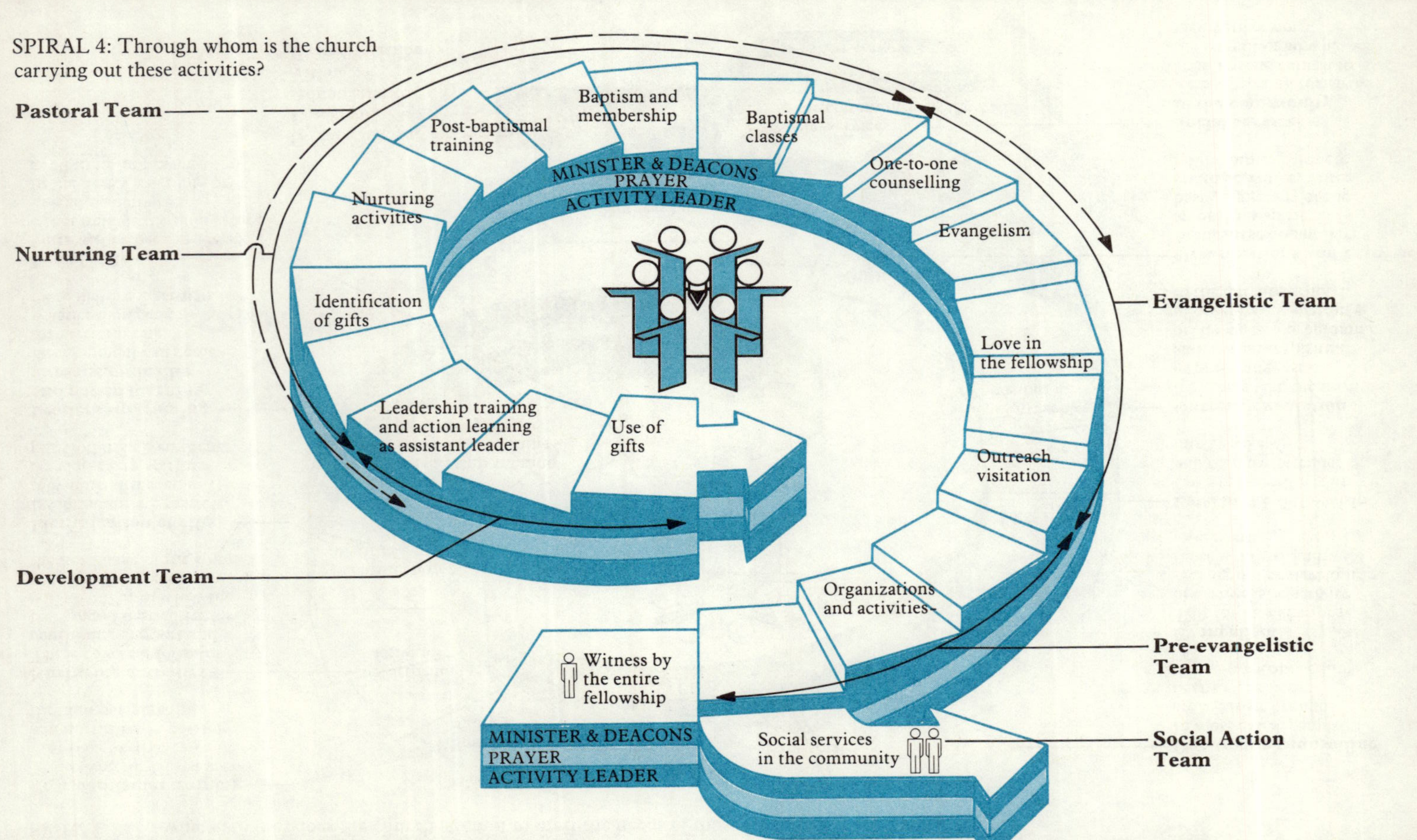

SPIRAL 4: Through whom is the church carrying out these activities?
Pastoral Team
Nurturing Team
Development Team
Evangelistic Team
Pre-evangelistic Team
Social Action Team
MINISTER & DEACONS
PRAYER
ACTIVITY LEADER
Post-baptismal training
Baptism and membership
Baptismal classes
One-to-one counselling
Evangelism
Nurturing activities
Identification of gifts
Love in the fellowship
Leadership training and action learning as assistant leader
Use of gifts
Outreach visitation
Organizations and activities
Witness by the entire fellowship
Organizations and activities
Social services in the community
MINISTER & DEACONS
PRAYER
ACTIVITY LEADER

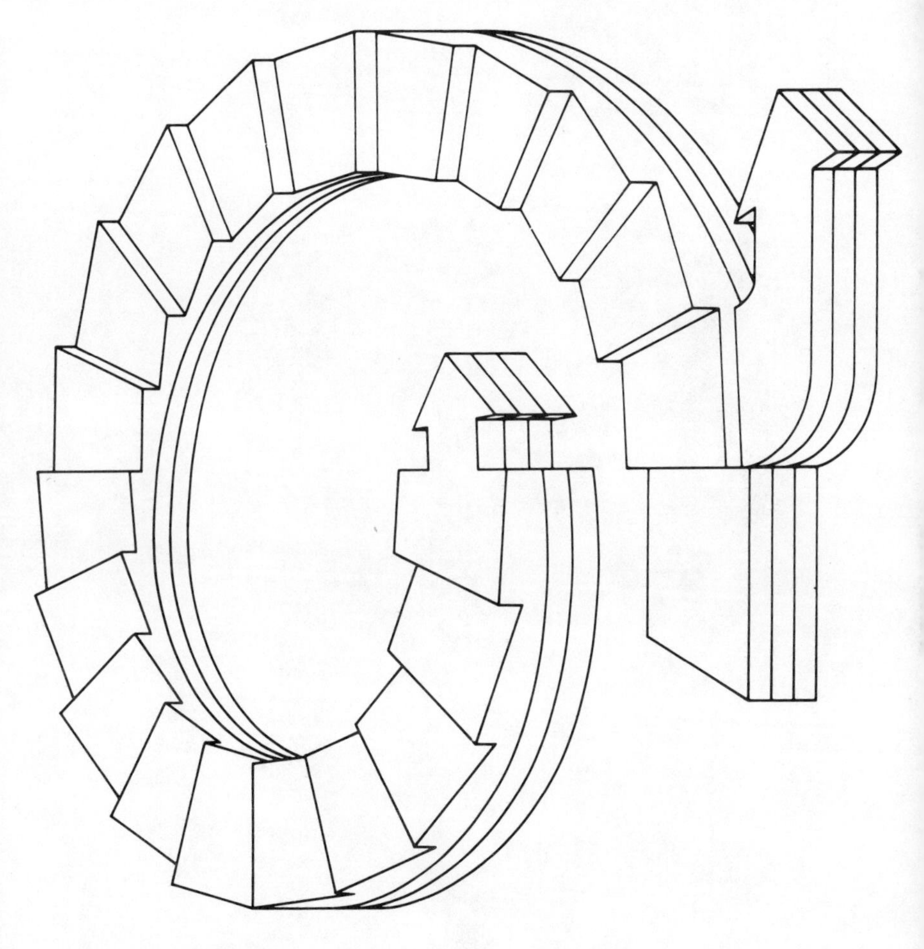

in the fellowship is a witness for good or ill, if only by the way he or she lives, or is seen to live, by the world outside.

The second point of interface is where individuals within the community become members of Christ's family. In the Baptist Church this involves baptism and membership. Possibly you may think it strange that we did not take conversion to be the point of transfer from the world into the Church. This is because we have remained faithful to Church Growth thinking. Commitment to Christ involves commitment to his Church. Only where this has been expressed openly can we consider that full commitment to Christ has been made.

By drawing a vertical rule through these two points of interface between the church and the community, and then adding a convenient horizontal, we have divided those for whom the church is responsible into four groups for each of which there is a particular emphasis:
- Attracting and serving
- Converting
- Nurturing
- Developing

This can be seen more clearly on Spiral 2.

Attracting and serving

These are both consequences of members of the fellowship witnessing by their lives in the community at large. Although the two activities are to be found together in the same quadrant, they are not necessarily one and the same thing. We do not serve others merely in order to attract them into the church. Our Christian service is motivated above all by a desire to meet the need of our neighbour, whatever that need might be. Yet, at the same time, there can be no doubt that where any service is carried out in a spirit of Christlike obedience, it does attract.

This is a very important factor to understand. The constant cry from struggling churches is, 'What do we do to bring in new people?' This simple query seems so valid, yet it subtly deflects attention from what may be the more correct and painful question: 'Are we as a church and as individuals living lives which reflect Jesus's love and so show him to others?' If all Christians were concentrating on this aspect it would mean that a fellowship would naturally become attractive. If we want to bring others into Christ's family, we must not simply advertize the benefits or even the costs of membership. We must go further and make those benefits and costs into living realities which can be seen in the people who already belong.

Converting

'To evangelize is so to present Christ Jesus in the power of the Holy Spirit that men shall come to put their trust in God through him.' So said the Archbishops' Third Committee of Enquiry into the Evangelistic Work of the Church in 1918. This definition calls into question the number of a church's so-called evangelistic activities which genuinely come under the umbrella of evangelism. Our survey showed for instance that despite the abundance of work listed as having an evangelistic purpose, the number of those actually becoming Christians through all that activity was low. A young wives' fellowship may have evangelism as its intention, yet in reality it may be fulfilling more of a nurturing role for young Christians or be a social function in the community. Again, a Scout troop may be justified as being an evangelistic activity while more often it may simply be a service to the community.

Nurturing

The Christians in the fellowship need to be nurtured and built up in their faith. When we come to faith in Christ, we are born again. Just as in the natural world a baby needs constant care and attention, so too in the spiritual world a newcomer should not be left to fend for himself. However, not only new Christians need nurturing, but also those who have forgotten their first love, and even those who are walking close to God. The process of growing up to their measure of the stature of the fullness of Christ (Ephesians 4.13) never ceases.

70

Developing

Through his Spirit, Christ has given gifts to his people. Indeed, Scripture teaches us that each Christian has received his own special share (1 Peter 4.10; 1 Corinthians 12.7) and it is up to every fellowship to identify those gifts and develop them. In that way each individual can see himself used more effectively in the Lord's service. This should lead to a conscious, continuous, creative process, not one where we wait for a job to become apparent and then look around to see who can best fill it. This is poor stewardship. We are failing the Lord if we do not use all the gifts he has provided.

Obviously, some activities in the life of a church will have more than one goal. Yet even these need consideration as to whether the stated objectives are being met in the best possible way by this single activity. It is also far too easy to become clouded in our thinking as to the purpose of the various activities in which we are involved. The spiral makes it possible to focus our objectives more sharply and to ask the questions that must be faced.

We next had to examine, '*By what activities does the church attempt to meet the needs of those for whom it is responsible?*' (Spiral 3) To do this we marked on the perimeter of this third spiral those activities which have a specific primary purpose. These we linked to the first of the spirals on which we had placed the people for whom the church is responsible. We tried to relate the activities to the people as closely as possible. Again, this revealed a progression in the spiritual nature of the activity right round the spiral.

We also recognized that there are two activities which had a bearing on the whole of the spiral. These are prayer and the Sunday services. No matter what the stage of spiritual development of those taking part in a particular activity, they can be supported and stimulated by prayer. For this reason we included a strand of prayer which runs through the diagram.

In a similar way, the Sunday services also have a contribution to make throughout the spiral. It is to be hoped that every member of the congregation can unite in the acts of worship as the church celebrates its faith, and in so doing gains a fresh sense of God's presence. However, not every function around the spiral can be included in each service. But it should be possible to develop an overall pattern of content and emphasis that relates to every section of the spiral over a number of weeks. Consideration of the needs of a church, as revealed through the spiral, may enable a minister to focus his services more selectively.

A slave for Christ
Central to all are a number of activities which have the convenient acronym of SLAVE. The activities are:

> **S**timulation and support
> **L**eadership
> **A**dministration
> **V**ision
> **E**xecutive action.

This, too, is shown as a strand running throughout the spiral.

Many ministers may feel that this **SLAVE** applies to themselves! But we have taken it to apply to the combined and recognized leadership of a local church, most usually expressed in a Baptist church in the minister and the deacons. The only body with pastoral oversight for the whole of the fellowship's life is its diaconate. Baptists will at once recognize that here an element of tension is introduced. For on the one hand we talk of the minister and deacons exercising leadership, yet on the other this leadership is subject to the Church Meeting. The Church Meeting for Baptists is 'the occasion when, as individuals and as a community, we submit ourselves to the guidance of the Holy Spirit and stand under the judgement of God that we may know what is the mind of Christ.' In human terms it is the ultimate decision-making body in the church. The deacons and minister are servants of the Church Meeting. However, it would seem that the interests of the Church Meeting are best served where the deacons and minister are providing the king of pastoral leadership which is conducive to Church Growth.

As well as providing general pastoral oversight for the church, the minister and deacons supply the dimensions of vision and leadership, and assume responsibility for the overall finance, fabric, administration and forward planning. It is from this central point that the vision of leadership permeates to the whole organization of a church, stimulating and supporting all the activities. It is also the central point to which these activities look for resources in the widest sense, as they need them, and for action as it is necessary.

Having reached this point in our thinking we went on to consider '*Through whom is the church carrying out these activities?*' (Spiral 4) It is here that the severe limitations of a one-man ministry come most sharply into focus. How could an individual, however gifted, possibly hope to fulfil all the functions necessary to meet the needs of all the people?

Even if he had the ability, which is unlikely, he would inevitably run short of both time and energy. This, in itself, speaks volumes in helping to explain why one man reaches his limit at around the 150 – 175 member mark.

The most obvious approach to breaking the one-man bottleneck is for the work to be shared. Perhaps this can best be done by the use of teams of gifted and trained people. Each team would have its own specific area of responsibility yet they would all link in together to be truly effective. On Spiral 4 you can see the way we responded to the situation at Altrincham. The whole idea is developed more fully in chapter seven, but the diagram shows that often there can be no clear cut-off point where one team's responsibility ends and another's begins.

In addition to the social action, pre-evangelistic, evangelistic, nurturing and development teams we have formed a pastoral team which can respond to the personal, and possibly very deep, needs of individuals within the fellowship. This is the team that tackles the in-depth problems of care and counselling of individuals. The work of these teams is discussed more fully in the next chapter.

I must stress that in showing how we responded to our own situation, I am not laying this out as a blueprint for every situation. Far from it. We reached our own conclusions with some difficulty and over an extended period of time. Any church which wants to take seriously the lessons of the survey and the spiral will need to go through its own thinking and praying process in order to find out what is right for its specific situation.

Our statement of the mission of a church together with the first three spirals can be applied very broadly. But when it comes to looking at the way an individual church will carry out these functions or will share the load, then it may be necessary to change some details or shift the balance of emphasis. The solution will almost certainly be quite different from that shown in the fourth spiral which relates to our own situation.

So, after much thought and prayer, we had plotted a scheme for growth, but what would happen when we put it into practice? There was only one way to find out.

HIGH WATERMARKS
- The emphasis for a church in its work should be to make disciples and add to the Lord's family, not simply to increase the membership.
- The spiral reflects this shift of emphasis and enables a church to think through its role and its activities with greater clarity.
- The spiral also emphasizes the need to develop leaders internally rather than relying on them arriving by transfer.

Chapter 7

Team games

PRACTISE WHAT YOU PREACH

Talking about Church Growth, and even planning for it, does not guarantee that things will change. We have already mentioned that while the majority of growing churches were observing some, if not all, of those Seven Vital Signs, so were some of the non-growing churches, though to a lesser extent. The inference from this was clear. However helpful these Vital Signs may be in stimulating growth, they cannot guarantee growth in themselves.

One additional factor clearly distinguishes growing churches from non-growing ones. It is the question of faith. Growing churches seem to be those, predominantly, that are expecting great things from God and have that conviction underlying all their activity. Church Growth is not simply doing the right things at the right time. It is also a matter of being a fellowship which believes that it is God's plan for his Church to grow and having the conviction that he wants it to happen in that particular church: it becomes a matter of faith.

With that in mind, I faced the Annual General Meeting of our church in May 1979. I had studied Church Growth in America and with Alan had carried out a survey into

Baptist church life. What is more, in Altrincham we had tried to put our findings into practice. But all this was not enough. I emphasized one particularly challenging aspect of Church Growth thinking. A church must want to grow and be willing to pay the cost. And that cost can be seen in terms of prayer and effort as well as finance. But, if people wish to see God's Kingdom extended, then they must be prepared to pay the price.

Thank God that in Altrincham the fellowship was willing to give itself whole-heartedly to this. But willingness is not enough, and we were not completely without disagreements as people expressed very genuine concern and misgivings over certain aspects of the plan. However, we worked together, and a year later I was able to tell the meeting that we seemed to be seeing signs of the numerical and spiritual growth we all desperately desired. Numerically, it was particularly encouraging. The graph which had been plateauing out was on the upturn again. (Fig. 20)

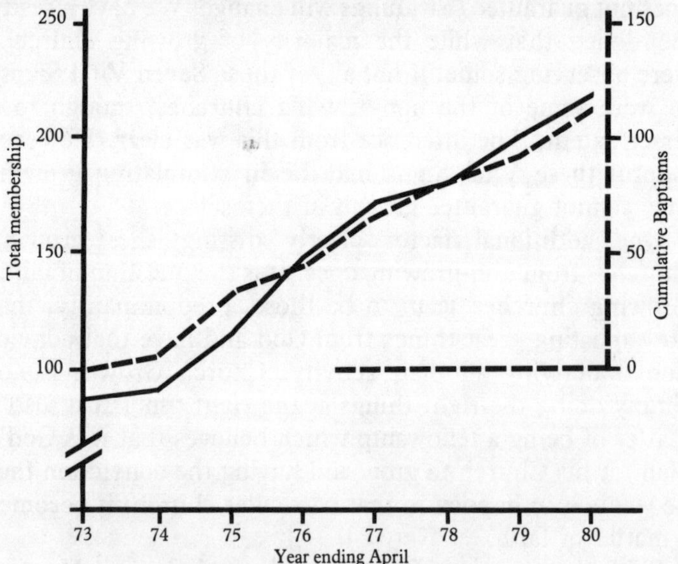

Fig. 20 Membership and cumulative baptisms by years

And spiritually, too, we had been making advances. The

76

spiral had been put into action and had produced positive results. In fact, over a two-year period, there has been a marked increase in activities connected with spiritual development, and we were already a church which had a firmly established structure of fellowship or cell groups. This was to be extended, particularly amongst the young people, who set up their own Bible study groups. These obviously served a useful purpose, providing a framework for fellowship and discussion. But at the same time, deeper, more systematic Bible study was needed and we have now established a cycle of home groups alternating with an expository Bible study for the whole fellowship, followed by prayer in small groups.

Our spiral theories worked in practice. They can work for you, too, and Spiral 5 enables you to map out your own specific needs and activities. From this it is possible to identify the gaps in your activities. In addition, you can look at the activities which are serving more than one purpose, checking to make sure that there is an overall balance to the work.

It is also important to see a balance of activity right around the spiral. Gaps could indicate an inherent weakness that might affect the longer term future. The correct balance for Altrincham would obviously not be exactly the same as for any other church. The situation is dependent on the age and spiritual needs of a church's own members and those on the fringe of the fellowship.

For us, identifying the gaps in activities proved to be a humbling experience. Firstly, we became acutely aware that we had very little – if anything – going on in the Development section of the spiral. Like so many other apparently successful churches, we were relying on leadership transferring in from outside, rather than training up our own members.

Secondly, we discovered that in comparison with what was happening in the Attracting and Nurturing sectors, we had very little going on in the Converting sector. We had plenty of activities which brought people onto church premises, but not many of these were actually designed to lead people to the point of commitment to Christ.

And our work amongst young people showed alarming gaps, with nothing really adequate for 11 – 14 year olds or for school leavers. Identifying the problems did not necessarily mean instant solutions but eventually we were able to meet the needs of both groups, setting up after-church meetings and other activities.

SLAVE LABOUR
As we began to turn theory into reality, one area which caused us much concern was the composition of the **SLAVE**, whose task it is to generate and stimulate the upward thrust of the spiral. Some time before beginning my research into Church Growth I had suggested the possibility of creating a small eldership. This had been rejected by my deacons, mainly because it would establish yet another tier within church life. A pastoral team functioning at the heart of the spiral was turned down for similar reasons. It was felt that it was the role of the deacons to lead and that they, with me, should form SLAVE.

With this basis in mind, it was possible to establish a number of ministry teams. In our church these teams have four common characteristics:

- Each is specifically task-oriented, concentrating on one particular sector of the spiral.
- Each is directly responsible to the Diaconate and through the Diaconate to the church meeting. This is helped by the fact that at least one member of each team is a deacon.
- Each team is headed by a lay person, who normally is a deacon. This structure positively encourages lay leaders to take the initiative. As pastor, I am merely an ex-officio member of each team.
- Each is compact in size. The teams are responsible for thinking and praying through possible courses for action, and not necessarily for the doing of the work themselves. Thus at present the Evangelistic Team is

78

composed of three members, but this does not mean that they are responsible for all the evangelism in the church! Similarly, the five members of the Social Action Team co-ordinate all the social work of the fellowship through other groups.

Initially, we had been thinking of three teams: an Evangelistic Team, a Pastoral Team and a Development Team.

While the names of the first two teams are self-explanatory, we need to define more clearly what we mean by the **Development Team**. It grew out of the planning group formed to think through the implications of the structure which we were establishing and helped me choose the leaders for the other teams. It is very small in number and will stay so. However, it now devotes considerable time to undertaking specific tasks within the fellowship. One was to go right through the list of members, allocating each person according to his gifts for possible work with one or other of the teams. It was also responsible for training programmes at all levels in the fellowship, from pre-baptismal preparation to guidance for team and group leaders.

But, as the Development Team worked together in seeking to identify and develop the gifts of the members, we began talking about five teams rather than three. These now are: social action, evangelistic, nurturing, development and pastoral. Perhaps it would now be helpful to set out here the tasks of the other four teams as they work in Altrincham. Again, we stress that this is only our solution and not in any way a rigid plan to follow.

The first and most urgent task of the **Pastoral Team** was to share my own burden and workload of counselling and general pastoring. The second was to co-ordinate the wider work of visiting the old, the housebound and those who were sick. The members of this team found themselves with a heavy work load, and so we have tried to relieve them of all other responsibilities within the fellowship. They also found the need to share with me, at quite a deep level, their concerns for those whom they were pastoring. The plan was for this small team to carry the main weight of personal counselling, but they were quite free to call on other members to help, particularly where specialized expertise such as legal, medical or practical advice was needed.

Identifying and meeting areas of social need within the community is the responsibility of the **Social Action Team**. Mostly this has been of a general nature and we recently issued newsletters detailing areas within the community where individual members of the church have been at work. None of these has been a big, spectacular project, but each represents an on-going commitment by the Women's and Men's Task Forces which were set up to reflect and express Christ's love in action, not only in the fellowship but also in the wider community.

The task of the **Evangelistic Team** is to encourage the church to 'by all means save some'. With this in mind the team has thought through, planned and initiated several ventures:

- Its members set up a discipleship training programme, aimed at leading men and women to Christ. In October 1979, three members of the church, including one member of the Evangelism Team, were sent for a week's training to an Evangelism Explosion Clinic. On their return they began a programme of visitation, during which other members are also being trained to share their faith.
- The team introduced an after-church event called Focus On Faith to which reasonably well-known personalities are invited in order to be questioned and so witness to the work of Christ in their lives.
- It has also engaged in an adventurous programme of publicizing the church, both through posters with lively slogans such as 'If you wouldn't be seen dead in church – come to life at ABC' at local railway stations, and through producing a community paper which is distributed four times a year to more than 5,000 homes in the area.
- Currently the team is planning a programme of home

visits to those who are on the very periphery of the church fellowship.

The **Nurturing Team** is largely made up of the leaders of the mid-week fellowship groups. Their main task is to select materials to be used in these groups and to discover together how best to encourage deeper relationships and a greater openness to the work of God among the members. Part of their role is also to train and develop further leaders for these fellowship groups.

TWELFTH MAN?

Putting the theory into action has also shown up the disadvantages. Being involved with the team meetings as an honorary member of each has taken up large amounts of my time and restricted my own programme of visiting. But where such meetings lead to definite action by a wider group of people than merely the minister, there can be no doubt as to their benefit, particularly where team leaders are doing much of the thinking and planning in preparation for the team activity.

In this way I have found that my role has shifted from that of being the one man who runs around trying to do everything, to the one who is trying to take seriously the need to 'prepare all God's people for the work of Christian service' (Ephesians 4.12).

It is true that we are still in the period of experimentation. The ministry teams have yet to settle into their role. But much valuable work has already been done, and it is exciting to see how we have been able to release many of the gifts of the fellowship for action. Nevertheless, despite sharing the work in this way and having begun to mobilize the members, there is still a great need for an increased level of participation.

MORE HANDS . . .

About two years ago, we formally agreed to seek to call 'someone to assist with pastoral care, whose prime responsibility would be for outreach, particularly among the young.' Yet while the team structure has moved positively ahead, it was some 15 months before we were able to find the right person to join us. In fact it was only in October 1980 that we welcomed Wyn Herd as our Pastoral Associate.

No doubt various human reasons could be given for the delay in finding a second member of staff. One reason must be the very structure of Baptist church life. With most English Baptist churches having a relatively weak financial base, an assistantship or curacy is generally not possible. In particular, gifted young men usually wish to proceed straight from theological college to full pastoral charge of a church of their own.

However, in this delay it is possible to see the hand of God. At the drawing board stage, it had been much easier to agree upon a job specification for an assistant than on the way the ministry teams should be structured within the total church administration. Had we found an assistant minister swiftly, perhaps some of the pressure to share the leadership among the members would have been eased. Instead we have had to face up to the issues of lay leadership in a way that we might not otherwise have done.

It was probably also providential that there was initially a fair amount of resistance to the concept of having elders or a pastoral team. It meant that we didn't settle on the first structure to be proposed, so instead of finishing up with three teams we now have the five, whose multi-directional ministry covers the whole range of church life. We now also have that second full-time member of staff.

WHERE DO WE GO FROM HERE?
From all that has been said, it is clear that the Altrincham story is far from over. In many ways it has only just begun! Our multi-directional team ministry including the second full-time member has yet to prove what it can do in the long term. We have still to grow into a really sizeable church. So in the meantime I dream. I dream, for instance, of the day when the church will pass the high-water mark of 316 members recorded in the time of the Rev Cowell

Lloyd in 1917. I dream, too, of spiritual growth, when every member of the fellowship will be closely knit together. I dream of the day when all the gifts of the church will be fully operative and when together, as ministers and lay-people alike, we will form a united army for the Lord.

And why not dream? Is not dreaming a mark of the new age of the Spirit? (Acts 2.17). I believe that God wants us to do great things in his service – it all depends on our vision.

HIGH WATERMARKS
- Each church will have to work out for itself how it can, under God's guidance, widen and share the total ministry of that church.
- This entails delegation, the giving and accepting of responsibility, within a framework of spiritual unity.
- The minister's role is clearly the most transformed, and shifts from being 'the minister' to that of leader and pastor to the wider ministry.

Chapter 8

Not really an apologia

FULL AND FRANK

Writing a book based primarily on the experiences of one church is a dangerous undertaking. For reasons of space alone, much must be left unsaid, leading to a real danger of creating misunderstanding. Because of this I want to use the final section of this book to clear up any wrong impressions that could have arisen.

It would be a shame if the reader were to put the book down with the impression that Altrincham Baptist Church were the ideal church and that various steps we have taken should be followed exactly. It would be a pity, too, if the book suggested that this is the only way in which a church can grow and that the spiral principle must be rigidly adhered to. This is far from the case. In Altrincham we have proved the value of this method, and it has seemed important to share our findings with others. God has blessed us and shown us how we as a fellowship should proceed. We believe that he can use our experiences to help others.

We are concerned above all with principles and priorities. The mission and the spiral are broadly valid for every church although their outworking will vary. Each individual situation is going to be different and churches must analyze their own case. Some will be big enough to support as many ministry teams as we have at Altrincham, or even more, whilst others may see different priorities.

ENDS OR MEANS?
Bigger and better churches are all very well, but when Church Growth in itself becomes the goal something has gone wrong somewhere. In secular terms it has been said that 'profit is not an end in itself but merely the reward of good management'. In the same way growth should be the consequence rather than the objective of the Great Commission.

Nor should the main concern be about numbers or certainly not numbers on the membership roll. The emphasis should be on the numbers of folk being won for Christ and being baptized into membership of his Church. It is true that we are concerned for numbers. We must know how our church is developing. The early church itself showed just this concern. Even on the day of Pentecost, someone among the disciples kept a cool enough head to count and record how many were converted. But my absolute conviction is that numerical growth can only ever be one side of the coin. The other side must be spiritual growth. And the two must go together.

The difficulty in creating a balance between the two stems from the fact that numerical growth is easily measured, while spiritual growth is much more difficult to evaluate. However, one of the greatest challenges of my ministry – if not the greatest – is how to lead people into a deeper knowledge and experience of the Lord.

TRUE VITALITY
Above all, I want to underline my conviction that it can never be right to take a mechanistic approach to Church Growth. If this book has given the impression that the key is simply to observe the Seven Vital Signs of Peter Wagner, and to introduce the concept of spirals and multi-directional ministry teams, then I have failed to make my point. In

86

those terms this book is not intended as a manual for success.

The key to growth is the Holy Spirit of God himself. 'You will succeed, not by military might or by your own strength, but by my spirit' (Zechariah 4.6). Ultimately, Church Growth is a spiritual phenomenon: it cannot be manipulated by techniques. The Vital Signs put forward by Peter Wagner and the principle of the spiral are no more than sails in which we hope to catch the wind of the Spirit. And remember that Jesus said, 'The wind blows wherever it wishes' (John 3.8). We cannot regulate the Spirit. Our job is to open up the fullest possible area of sail in order to move ahead at maximum power.

When I first came to Altrincham, I was conscious of walking into a situation that had already been prepared by the Spirit of God. I was no more than a catalyst in a God-given situation. Our Church Growth studies have confirmed how true this is. The key factor which distinguishes growing churches from those which are not growing seems ultimately to be that spiritual intangible faith. Peter Wagner talks of optimism, together with obedience and pragmatism, as characterizing the Church Growth mood. As a Baptist I warm to this. It's what Carey felt all those years ago. God can and will help us, if only we trust him.

Faith then is so much more than mere expectancy. We see this clearly in the story of the epileptic boy (Matthew 17.14–21). The disciples expected success; they expected to be able to heal the boy. Indeed, not only had Jesus given them authority over 'evil spirits' (Matthew 10.1), they had apparently already had some success in meeting men in their need (Luke 10.17). So why did they fail? Is it possible that they had become over-confident, over-confident in the sense that they had come to place their confidence in themselves and not in God? Our confidence cannot be in ourselves – but rather in the God who raised the Lord Jesus from the dead, who poured out his Spirit on all mankind and who continues to do so.

HIGH WATERMARKS
- Making disciples under God's guidance should be our aim: Church Growth will be a consequence.
- It is God through his Holy Spirit who grows the church.
- We must put our faith in God and in his work.

Appendix 1

Bibliography

AMERICAN CHURCH GROWTH MATERIAL

Charles L. Chaney & Ron S. Lewis: *Design for Church Growth* (Broadman Press, Nashville, Tennessee 1978)

Harvie M. Conn (Ed): *Theological Perspectives on Church Growth* (Presbyterian & Reformed Publishing Co., Nutley, New Jersey 1976)

Orlando E. Costas: *The Church and Its Mission* (Tyndale, Wheaton, Illinois 1975) Contains a theological critique.

Vergil Gerber: *God's Way to Keep a Church Going and Growing* (Regal Books, Glendale, California 1973)

Dan Martin: 'Off the top of the charts . . . The 425 fastest growing churches in the Southern Baptist Convention – and why they've grown' (Home Missions, December 1977)

Donald McGavran: *Understanding Church Growth* (Eerdmans, Grand Rapids, Michigan 1970)

Donald McGavran & Wyn Arn: *How to Grow a Church: Conversations About Church Growth* (Regal Books, Glendale, California 1973)

Robert H. Schuller: *Your Church Has Real Possibilities* (Regal Books, Glendale, California 1975)

Howard A. Snyder: *New Wineskins* (Marshall, Morgan and Scott, London 1977)

Alan R. Tippett: *Church Growth and the Word of God* (Eerdmans, Grand Rapids, Michigan 1970)

C. Peter Wagner: *Your Church Can Grow: Seven Vital Signs of a Healthy Church* (Regal Books, Glendale, California 1976)
Your Spiritual Gifts Can Help Your Church Grow (Regal Books, Glendale, California 1976)
Our Kind of People (John Knox Press, Atlanta, Georgia 1979)

C. Peter Wagner and others: *Various work books published during 1970s* (Department of Church Growth, Fuller Evangelistic Association, Box 989, Pasadena, California 91102)

Lausanne Occasional Paper: No. 1: The Pasadena Consultation Homogeneous Unit Principle (Wheaton, Illinois 1977)

BRITISH CHURCH GROWTH MATERIAL

Eddie Gibbs: *Urban Church Growth: Clues from South America and Britain* (Grove Books, Bramcote, Notts. 1977)
Grow Through Groups (Grove Books, Bramcote, Notts. 1979)
Body Building Exercises for the Local Church (Falcon, London 1979)
I Believe in Church Growth (To be published by Hodder & Stoughton in 1981)

Martin Goldsmith: *Can My Church Grow?* (Hodder & Stoughton, London 1980)

Jeffrey Harris and Peter Jarvis: *Counting to Some Purpose* (The Methodist Church: Home Mission Division, London 1979)

Signs of Hope: An examination of the numerical and spiritual state of churches in membership with the Baptist Union of Great Britain and Ireland (Baptist Publications, London 1979)

Robin Thomson: *Can British Churches Grow? A Workbook*
   (Bible & Medical Missionary Fellowship, 186 Kennington Park Road, London SE11 4BT, London 1978)

FOR ANALYSIS AND RESEARCH
Currie, Gilbert & Horsley: *Churches and Churchgoers*
   (Oxford: Clarendon Press 1977)
David Wasdell: *Tools for the Task: Growth in Context* Urban
   Church Project, St. Matthias Vicarage, Poplar High
   Street, London E14 0AE

American Church Growth Books obtainable in Britain from
Evangelical Missionary Alliance, 186 Kennington Park
Road, London SE11 4BT

No. of questionnaire

____

This sheet will be separated from the rest of the question-naire when the results are being analysed and only the number above will be used for identification purposes at that stage.

Name and address
of church: _______________________

Name and address
of respondent: _______________________

Office of
respondent:

	Minister	Full-time assistant ministers	
Name		A________ B________	
Age		A	B
How long in the ministry		A________ B________	
Ministerial training at		A________	
		B________	
How long at this church		A________ B________	
Any special pastoral responsibility		A________	
		B________	

If you have any part-time ministers, lay assistants, associate pastors, etc. or team and shared ministries, could you please outline below?

____

____

If there is no minister, how long is it since the departure of the last one? _______________________

No. of questionnaire

Section A – The Community which the Church serves

1 How would you describe the area in which the church is situated?

inner city__________   city fringe__________

suburban__________   large town(50,000 plus)__________

rural__________   small town(under 50,000)__________

2 What is the population of the area approximately?

3 Is the congregation mainly local or drawn from a larger area?

mainly local__________   half and half__________

mainly non-local__________

4 How many other Christian churches are there within a radius of three miles?__________

5 How many of these have a strong evangelical emphasis?

6 Please fill in this table to describe (a) the housing in the area as a whole, and (b) the housing occupied by your fellowship. In each column mark with the number 1 the predominant type of local housing, 2 the next most common, and so on for all types which apply.

	the local area as a whole	housing occupied by your fellowship
Spacious detached		
Detached private		
Semi-detached		
Terrace housing		
High rise flats		
Low rise flats (up to 3 storeys)		
Other (please specify)		

94

7 Please fill in this table to describe (a) the kinds of secondary education available in the area, and (b) the kinds of schools attended by the children of your Fellowship. TICK ALL WHICH APPLY.

	Schools available in the local area	Schools attended by children of the church
Comprehensive		
Secondary modern		
Grammar		
Independent (day school)		
Independent (boarding)		
Other – please specify		

8 Do most of the children in the church stay at school or college till 18?

most___________   some___________

few or none___________

9 Do many of them go to University?

most___________   some___________

few or none___________

10 Is part of the local population from the new Commonwealth?

yes___________   no___________

11 If 'yes', which part?

West Indies___________   Asia___________

Other (please specify)___________

12 What proportion of your congregation is from this section of the community? Place a (c) opposite the appropriate percentage below. Then place a (p) for the proportion of the local population which comes from the new Commonwealth.

0–20%___________   21–40%___________

41–60%___________   61–80%___________

81–100%___________

13 To what extent is your church active in meeting the social needs of the community?

————————very————————reasonably————————under————————scarcely

95

14 Please fill in this table to describe (a) the occupations of the local population as a whole, (b) the occupations of the members of your fellowship, and (c) the occupations of your Deacons. In each column mark with the number 1 the predominant group, with 2 the next most common, and so with all groups which apply.

	The local population as a whole	Occupations of your fellowship	Occupations of your Deacons
Employers & Managers			
Professional			
Foreman/Supervisor			
Skilled workers			
Unskilled workers			
Farmers & agricultural workers			
Office/clerical			
Other – please specify			

15 Do most of the people in your area work locally?

yes_____________   no_____________

half and half_____________

16. What proportion of your members are blue collar workers?_______%

17 What proportion of your members would you regard as being definitely at the top end of the social/income scale? _________%

18 Has the composition of the population in the surrounding neighbourhood stayed much the same or changed in any way during the last 5 years? (e.g. occupations, races, age groups)

stayed the same_____________   changed_____________

If it has changed please describe the groups of people who have come to the area or left.

____

____

19 Has the neighbourhood been declining or developing during this time?

declining_____________   developing_____________

stayed the same_____________

Section B – Activities Associated with the Church

1 Please tick in each column as appropriate.

	Activities for which the buildings are used	Activities for which the church accepts the responsibility	Activities which the church sees as an important part of its outreach
Brownies			
Girl Guides			
Cubs			
Boy Scouts			
Housing trusts for aged, blind, or those recovered from ill health, etc.			
Welfare services			
One-parent families			
Mothers & toddlers			
Play groups			
Alcoholics Anon			
Badminton			
Amateur dramatics			
Socials			
Local societies			
Others – please specify			

Section C – The General Organizational Life of the Church

1 Could you please fill in the following chart concerning the regular Activities in your fellowship? Gaps have been left at several points in the chart in case you have more than one example of a particular activity.

For notes on completing this page, see opposite.

The event or activity	frequency	average attendance	number of leaders	purpose ***
1 Sunday School				
2 Boy Covenanters				
3 Girl Covenanters				
4 Women's meetings				
5				
6 Men's meetings				
7				
8 Bible study groups				
9				
10				
11				
12 Church meeting				
13 Church night				
14 House groups				
15				
16				
17 Youth club				
18 Boy's Brigade				
19 Girl's Brigade				
20 Coffee Bar				
21				
22 Other – please specify				
23				
24				
25				

Notes for completion of the table on the previous page.

* In activities 2 and 3 we have used the term Covenanters. We appreciate that this is not a term of overall use, but we would ask you to interpret it loosely in terms of teenage activity which has some spiritual content, e.g. Christian Endeavour.

** We would also ask you to interpret the term 'house group' loosely to cover small regular meetings of members of the fellowship in private homes. We ask more questions about such groups as to their purpose later in the questionnaire.

*** In the last column, could you please indicate by the letters a, b, or c, whether you regard the purpose of each activity as primarily: a – a social service, b – nurturing of the existing fellowship, or c – evangelistic in purpose.

Questions of Section C Continued:-

2 Is your church an open or closed membership?

open____________   closed____________

3 How many Deacons do you have?______

4 How many Elders do you have?______

5 How do you differentiate their roles?

6 How often do they meet?

deacons____________   elders____________

7 How many Deacons elected in the last three years became Deacons for the first time?______

8 Would you say the theological position of your members is predominantly

conservative evangelical____________   charismatic____________

middle-of-the-road Baptist____________   radical____________

other – please specify____________

9 Would you say the theological position of the minister is

conservative evangelical____________   charismatic____________

middle-of-the-road Baptist____________   radical____________

other – please specify____________

10 What do you consider the particular strength of your minister to be? Please number in order, with 1 for the strongest.

preaching___________   pastoral care___________

administration___________   vision/leadership___________

11 In the activities listed in Question 1 of this Section, which involve music?   Please tick.

1	2	3	4	5	6	7	8	9	10	11	12	13	14	15	16	17	18	19	20	21	22	23	24	25

12 Do you have regular music other than piano or organ?

13 If so, what? And when is it used?

14 Do you use anything other than the Baptist Hymn Book frequently in your services?

Praise for Today___________   Sounds of Living Water___________

Youth Praise___________   Psalm Praise___________

Have produced your___________   Other – please specify___________
own collection

15 What proportion of your members are Charismatic?

0–20%___________   21–40%___________

41–60%___________   61–80%___________

81–100%___________

16 Do they meet separately?

yes___________   no___________

17 What is their general influence?

unifying___________   divisive___________

stimulating___________   other – please specify___________

18 Do you have services regularly when members of the fellowship are particularly asked to bring along an outside friend?

no___________   yes___________

monthly___________   quarterly___________

other & specify___________

19 Do you have family services – i.e. those when the children stay in for the whole of the service?

no____________	quarterly____________
monthly____________	weekly____________
only on special occasions____________	morning____________
evening____________	

20 Does the minister often make appeals for members of the congregation to come forward in witness?

yes____________   no____________

only on particular occasions – please____________
                              specify

21 Do you serve tea or coffee after services?

	never	always	occasionally
mornings			
evenings			

22 Do strangers tend to stay for the tea or coffee?

yes____________   no____________

23 Do you have a system for inviting strangers to lunch or tea after services?

yes____________   no____________

24 How many regular prayer groups do you have? (as distinct from fellowship groups – see D 9)____________ groups

25 What is the average attendance?____________

26 How is the membership organized?

by geographical area____________	by alphabetical list____________
by age____________	by compatibility____________
by self-selection____________	open to anyone____________

27 Do you have lay participation in services? How often? What do they do?

no____________	always____________
frequently____________	regularly____________
occasionally____________	leading prayer?____________
reading?____________	
witness?____________	
greeting during service?____________	other – please specify?____________

28 What is your approximate total annual income? £_____

29 Do you work on an all-in budget basis?

yes_____________   no_____________

30 What is the average weekly offertory? £_______

31 Do you arrange general fund-raising activities such as sales of work or coffee mornings?

yes_____________   no_____________

32 What proportion of total income do you give to Christian causes outside the local church and area?

at home___________%   overseas___________%

33 Do you encourage tithing?

yes_____________   no_____________

34 How much regular secretarial assistance does your minister get each week?

none_____________   days_____________

hours_____________

35 What equipment do you have?

typewriters?_____________   duplicators?_____________

Addressograph?_____________   other?_____________

36 What audio-visual equipment do you have?

TV camera_____________   VCR_____________

cine camera_____________   projector_____________

tape recorder_____________

Section D – Pastoral Care

1 How are new guests or people who visit for the first time received or welcomed into the fellowship?

visitor's book___________   card to fill in___________

other – please specify___________

2 Do you have a programme of follow-up?

no___________   yes___________   If yes:

by post___________   visit by minister___________

lay visitor___________   other – please specify___________

3 Do you have a programme for nurturing new members to the church, and/or to the Christian life?

no___________   yes___________

by study group___________   by church friend___________

by fellowship group___________

4 Who is responsible for the pastoral care in the church?

the minister___________   the Deacons___________

a wider group___________

5 How many people in your church see pastoral care as a substantial part of their personal ministry?

number of people___________

6 Do Deacons or Elders have pastoral oversight of a section of the fellowship?

	yes	no
elders		
deacons		

7 How is the section allocated?

by the minister___________   by geographical area___________

by age___________   by compatibility___________

by fellowship group___________

8 Is there a regular pastoral team of visitors?

yes___________   no___________

9 To what extent do cells or small fellowship groups play a part in the pastoral care in your church?

major______________ considerable______________

some______________ minor______________

10 How often do such groups meet?

monthly______________ fortnightly______________

weekly______________ occasionally______________

11 Where do they meet?

church______________ group leader's home______________

other home______________ always the same location______________

by rotation______________ by invitation______________

12 How would you define their purpose?

nurturing______________ Bible study______________

evangelistic______________ general discussion______________

prayer emphasis______________ primarily social______________

13 What is the average size?______

14 How long have they been functioning?

____

____

15 How do the people join together in such groups, or are they selected?

by the minister______________ by geographical area______________

by compatibility______________ by personal choice______________

other – please specify______________ by age______________

16 By what means are the wider body of members involved in pastoral care?

visitation______________ literature distribution______________

flower distribution______________ task force to help aged and infirm______________

church friend system______________ other – please specify______________

17 Do you have a local education grant for youth work?

yes______________ no______________

18 Do you have a full-time youth worker? or leader?

yes______________ no______________

104

19 Do you run a tape ministry?

yes_____________   no_____________

20 Or a telephone ministry?

yes_____________   no_____________

21 Do you feel the church exercises pastoral care of the membership as successfully as 5 years ago?

about the same_____________   more successfuly_____________

less successfully_____________

If more successfully how have the methods of pastoral care been changed?

____

____

____

____

22 Are there more or fewer lay people than 5 years ago who could assist with pastoral care and leadership in the church?

more_____________   about the same_____________

fewer_____________

If 'more' or 'fewer', please describe the resource people who have been lost or gained.

____

____

____

____

____

Section E – Outreach

1 Please list the main activities in outreach by your church in the last five years

guest services___________   holiday club___________

missions___________   gospel concerts___________

other – please specify___________

2 What is actually being done now?

____

____

____

____

3 Do you have a Committee especially responsible?

yes___________   no___________

4 Within the total activity of your church, can you list please the following in the order in which they take up time or effort? Use 1, 2, & 3 with 1 for the maximum.

outreach___________   nurturing of the existing
fellowship___________

community service___________

5 How often are your services planned with outreach particularly in mind?

weekly___________   monthly___________

quarterly___________   occasionally___________

6 Do you carry out any particular programme of evangelism?

yes___________   no___________

7 If so which one – or more?

____

____

8 How many people are involved?

___________ in total of which___________ are lay

9 Do you have any form of regular literature distribution?

yes___________   no___________

10 How many people are involved?

Number of people___________

11 How many people in the last five years have been won for Christ?

______in total of which the following have been won

______through youth work, ______through normal pastoral care,

______through Sunday School and then church, ______through special missions,

and ______through evangelistic programmes.

12 Are you a member of the Council of Churches?

yes______________   no______________

13 Do you take part in

united services?______________   united missions?______________

united house groups?______________

14 Do you run, say, a Saturday morning 'shoppers' coffee bar?

yes______________   no______________

15 Or an evangelistic coffee bar for young people?

yes______________   no______________

16 How would you define church growth?

____

____

____

17 Do you wish to grow in numbers?

yes______________   no______________

18 How many extra people could you handle? (Please ring appropriate number)   25 / 50 / 100 / 150 / 200

19 What limitations do you see, and why?

____

____

20 What fruits of growth can you identify within your church during the last five years? ______________________

____

21 What is presenting further growth at present? ______

____

22 Around what issues does stress or conflict arise in your church? ____

____

Section F – Data on the Church

1. Can you please break down the present membership in the following table:

	Membership		Total Fellowship	
	Male	Female	Male	Female
Aged 0 – 15				
Aged 16 – 35				
Aged 36 – 55				
Aged 56 plus				

2. What are the present numbers attending church?

	Sunday morning	Sunday p.m.	Sunday School
Men			
Women			
Children			
What time do you meet?			

3. Could you give the following historical data?

	10 years	5 years	2 years	now
Membership of the church				
Total fellowship of the church				
Membership of the Sunday School				

4. Can you classify those joining or leaving the fellowship in recent years? To simplify the completion of the following table, we have made the individual headings consistent with the return which you make each January to your Association.

(continued on next page)

	1969	1970	1971	1972	1973	1974	1975	1976	1977	1978
Additions by baptism										
Additions by transfer										
Additions by profession										
Deletions by death										
Deletions by transfer										
Deletions – other causes										

5. Do the buildings meet the present needs of the church?

yes________________   no________________

6. If 'no' what alterations would you like to see and why?

____

____

____

____

____

____

____

Geographic Distribution of Sample

	No. of churches in area	No. of churches sent questionnaire	Churches completing questionnaire	
			Total no. of churches	No. of churches growing
Bedfordshire & S. Hunts	40	8	6	6
Berkshire	39	13	7	6
Bristol & District	64	23	15	9
Buckinghamshire	33	5	5	4
Cambridgeshire	43	7	3	1
Devon & Cornwall	78	19	13	9
East Midlands	190	52	31	15
Essex	75	26	15	9
Glos. & Herefordshire	49	10	6	4
Hertfordshire	43	13	3	3
Home Counties	20	8	4	4
Kent	63	23	14	12
Lancashire & Cheshire	168	53	34	17
London	262	107	61	29
Norfolk	35	9	3	2
Northamptonshire	67	12	5	3
Northern	38	11	7	6
Oxon. & E. Glos.	41	7	6	5
Southern	85	30	18	9
Suffolk Union	29	7	4	2
Sussex	46	19	12	9
Western	31	7	7	2
West Midland	128	41	21	13
Wilts. & East Somerset	31	9	5	3
Worcestershire	23	6	2	1
Yorkshire	125	36	20	12